Media Center Discovery

180 Ready-to-Use
Activities for
Language Arts,
Grades 5–8

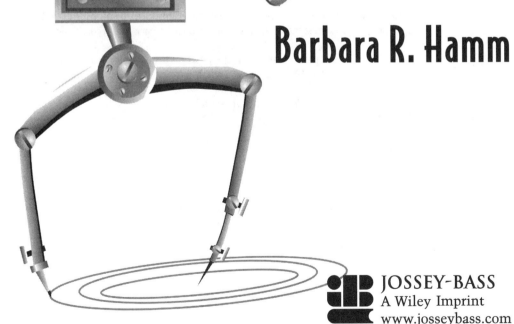

Barbara R. Hamm

 JOSSEY-BASS
A Wiley Imprint
www.josseybass.com

Published by Jossey-Bass
A Wiley Imprint
989 Market Street, San Francisco, CA 94103-1741   www.josseybass.com

Jossey-Bass books and products are available through most bookstores. To contact Jossey-Bass directly, call 888-378-2537 or fax to 800-605-2665, or visit our Website at www.josseybass.com.

Library of Congress Cataloging-in-Publication Data

Hamm, Barbara R.
      Media center discovery : 180 ready-to-use activities for
language arts, grades 5–8 / Barbara R. Hamm.—1st ed.
        p. cm.
      ISBN 0-7879-6960-5 (alk. paper)
      1. School libraries—Activity programs.   2. Library orientation
for school children.   3. Middle school education—Activity
programs.   4. Media programs (Education)   5. Libraries and
education.   I. Title.
Z675.S3H258 2004
027.8—dc22
                                                              2003026458

FIRST EDITION
PB Printing   10 9 8 7 6 5 4 3 2 1

Contents

....

UNIT ONE...

Getting to Know Your Library Media Center

UNIT ELEVEN ....

Using What You Have Learned: Writing and Publishing

Special thanks to my family: my husband, Edward; my daughter, Gina; my grandchildren, Ryan and Bridget; my son-in-law, Dan; and my Mother, who give me moral support in everything I do.

Thanks also to my students, who make teaching an enjoyable and memorable experience.

Introduction

....

Media Center Discovery was developed to assist librarians, computer specialists, and teachers in instructing students on how to use the library media center effectively. It is concise and straightforward, and uses techniques such as games and activities to reinforce the lessons. Collaboration is encouraged to develop independent research skills with a high degree of proficiency in both school and public libraries.

This book provides background information for each skill and resource. The lessons describe the different resources, how to use them, and how to choose the best ones to complete a project. Electronic resources and Internet skills are also included to expand the student's research capabilities.

Student learning levels are denoted as □ beginner, grades 3 and 4; ◪ intermediate, grades 5 and 6; and ■ advanced, grades 7 and 8. The symbols (□ ◪ ■) are used in the transparency and activity sections of each lesson description. Some students may be considered beginners in some skills even if they are advanced in grade level. The teacher may use an appropriate activity to accommodate the learning level. The beginner students are working on *basic* skills; the intermediate students are working on *proficiency;* and the advanced students are working to become *exemplary* as noted in the American Library Association (ALA) sequential literacy standards.

The lessons follow the ALA sequential skills and the information literacy standards for student learning. Readers can access the nine information standards for student learning at http://www.infolit.org/definitions/9standards.htm. To check your state's standards, access http://dir.yahoo.com/education/k_12/curriculum_Standards/By_Region/U_S__States. Type the state name as a key word and go to state education agencies.

This book is an essential resource for developing students who will become information literate and who will be able to access information efficiently and effectively (ALA Information Literacy Standards 1 through 3). Once these students become information literate, they will be able to pursue information related to personal interests, they will be able to appreciate literature and other creative expressions of information, and they will be able to strive for excellence in information seeking and knowledge generation (ALA Information Literacy Standards 4 through 6). Use of this book will encourage students to contribute positively to the learning community and to recognize the importance of information to a democratic society. It will encourage ethical behavior in regard to information and information technology. As positive contributors to the learning community and to society, students will participate effectively in groups to pursue and generate information (ALA Information Literacy Standards 7 through 9).

This book gathers information about print, nonprint, and electronic library materials. It fills a need to have readily accessible background material and Internet links. Each lesson contains a concise and complete instructional guide for teaching the lesson; work pages for student practice; and suggestions for projects to encourage collaboration among librarians, computer specialists, and classroom teachers.

As lifelong learners, students will broaden their knowledge from the school library to the public library and beyond. The focus is on the student. The intent and purpose of this book is to introduce, develop, and refine skills necessary for success in the learning environment.

The ALA Nine Information Literacy Standards for Student Learning . . . .

The American Association of School Librarians (AASL) and the Association for Education Communications and Technology (ACET) began a project in 1983 to set up guidelines for developing school library media programs. A four-member writing team and reactor panel served as the Standards Writing Committee. Association officers in each state had the opportunity to review drafts. The project was finished in 1988.

The guidelines' focus is on the building-level library media specialist, who is the link between the students, teachers, administrators, parents, and available resources. They emphasize stressing the specific and unique needs of the school curriculum to determine the type and level of the program offered. "The mission is to ensure that students and staff are effective users of ideas and information" (*Information Power, Guidelines for School Library Media Programs,* American Association of School Librarians and Association for Educational Communication and Technology, Copyright 1988).

To the Instructor

The standards can be found to some degree in every lesson. The ◆ symbol is used to show lessons that emphasize a standard.

Information Literacy

STANDARD 1: THE STUDENT WHO IS INFORMATION LITERATE *ACCESSES* INFORMATION EFFICIENTLY AND EFFECTIVELY.

◆ 1-A Library	◆ 2-C Index	◆ 3-B Dictionary
◆ 1-B Catalog	◆ 2-D Glossary	◆ 3-C Thesaurus
◆ 2-A Book Parts	2-E Bibliography	◆ 3-D Encyclopedia
◆ 2-B Contents	◆ 3-A Almanac	◆ 3-E Record Books

- 4-A Atlas
- 4-B Maps
- 4-C Gazetteer
- 5-A Biography
- 5-B Quotations
- 6-A Periodicals
- 6-B Newspapers
- 6-C Magazines
- 6-D Reader's Guide
- 6-E Vertical Files
- 6-F Outside
- 7-A Dewey

- 8-A Books
- 8-B Genres
- 8-C Myths
- 8-D Tall Tales
- 8-E Poetry
- 8-F Awards
- 8-G Book Reports
- 8-H Copyright
- 9-A Video
- 9-B Microfiche
- 10-A Search Engines
- 10-B Internet

- 10-C Software
- 10-D Word Processing
- 10-E Prod. Software
- 11-A Organization
- 11-B Self-Organization
- 11-C Topics
- 11-D Notes
- 11-E Prewrite
- 11-F Outline
- 11-G Timeline
- 11-H Draft
- 11-I Publish

STANDARD 2: THE STUDENT WHO IS INFORMATION LITERATE *EVALUATES* INFORMATION CRITICALLY AND COMPETENTLY.

- 1-A Library
- 1-B Catalog
- 2-A Book Parts
- 2-B Contents
- 2-C Index
- 2-D Glossary
- 2-E Bibliography
- 3-A Almanac
- 3-B Dictionary
- 3-C Thesaurus
- 3-D Encyclopedia
- 3-E Record Books
- 4-A Atlas
- 4-B Maps
- 4-C Gazetteer
- 5-A Biography

- 5-B Quotations
- 6-A Periodicals
- 6-B Newspapers
- 6-C Magazines
- 6-D Reader's Guide
- 6-E Vertical Files
- 6-F Outside
- 7-A Dewey
- 8-A Books
- 8-B Genres
- 8-C Myths
- 8-D Tall Tales
- 8-E Poetry
- 8-F Awards
- 8-G Book Reports
- 8-H Copyright

- 9-A Video
- 9-B Microfiche
- 10-A Search Engines
- 10-B Internet
- 10-C Software
- 10-D Word Processing
- 10-E Prod. Software
- 11-A Organization
- 11-B Self-Organization
- 11-C Topics
- 11-D Notes
- 11-E Prewrite
- 11-F Outline
- 11-G Timeline
- 11-H Draft
- 11-I Publish

STANDARD 3: THE STUDENT WHO IS INFORMATION LITERATE *USES* INFORMATION ACCURATELY AND CREATIVELY.

- 1-A Library
- 1-B Catalog
- 2-A Book Parts
- 2-B Contents
- 2-C Index

- 2-D Glossary
- 2-E Bibliography
- 3-A Almanac
- 3-B Dictionary
- 3-C Thesaurus

- 3-D Encyclopedia
- 3-E Record Books
- 4-A Atlas
- 4-B Maps
- 4-C Gazetteer

- ◆ 5-A Biography
- ◆ 5-B Quotations
- ◆ 6-A Periodicals
- ◆ 6-B Newspapers
- ◆ 6-C Magazines
- ◆ 6-D Reader's Guide
- ◆ 6-E Vertical Files
- ◆ 6-F Outside
- ◆ 7-A Dewey
- ◆ 8-A Books
- ◆ 8-B Genres

- ◆ 8-C Myths
- ◆ 8-D Tall Tales
- ◆ 8-E Poetry
- ◆ 8-F Awards
- ◆ 8-G Book Reports
- ◆ 8-H Copyright
- ◆ 9-A Video
- ◆ 9-B Microfiche
- ◆ 10-A Search Engines
- ◆ 10-B Internet
- ◆ 10-C Software

- ◆ 10-D Word Processing
- ◆ 10-E Prod. Software
- ◆ 11-A Organization
- ◆ 11-B Self-Organization
- ◆ 11-C Topics
- ◆ 11-D Notes
- ◆ 11-E Prewrite
- ◆ 11-F Outline
- ◆ 11-G Timeline
- ◆ 11-H Draft
- ◆ 11-I Publish

Independent Learning

STANDARD 4: THE STUDENT WHO IS AN INDEPENDENT LEARNER IS INFORMATION LITERATE AND *PURSUES* INFORMATION RELATED TO *PERSONAL INTERESTS*.

- ◆ 1-A Library
- ◆ 1-B Catalog
- ◆ 2-A Book Parts
- ◆ 2-B Contents
- ◆ 2-C Index
- ◆ 2-D Glossary
-   2-E Bibliography
- ◆ 3-A Almanac
- ◆ 3-B Dictionary
- ◆ 3-C Thesaurus
- ◆ 3-D Encyclopedia
- ◆ 3-E Record Books
- ◆ 4-A Atlas
-   4-B Maps
-   4-C Gazetteer
- ◆ 5-A Biography

- ◆ 5-B Quotations
- ◆ 6-A Periodicals
- ◆ 6-B Newspapers
- ◆ 6-C Magazines
-   6-D Reader's Guide
-   6-E Vertical Files
- ◆ 6-F Outside
- ◆ 7-A Dewey
- ◆ 8-A Books
- ◆ 8-B Genres
- ◆ 8-C Myths
- ◆ 8-D Tall Tales
- ◆ 8-E Poetry
- ◆ 8-F Awards
-   8-G Book Reports
-   8-H Copyright

- ◆ 9-A Video
-   9-B Microfiche
- ◆ 10-A Search Engines
- ◆ 10-B Internet
- ◆ 10-C Software
- ◆ 10-D Word Processing
- ◆ 10-E Prod. Software
-   11-A Organization
-   11-B Self-Organization
-   11-C Topics
-   11-D Notes
-   11-E Prewrite
-   11-F Outline
-   11-G Timeline
-   11-H Draft
- ◆ 11-I Publish

STANDARD 5: THE STUDENT WHO IS AN INDEPENDENT LEARNER IS INFORMATION LITERATE AND *APPRECIATES* LITERATURE AND OTHER CREATIVE EXPRESSIONS OF INFORMATION.

1-A Library	5-B Quotations	◆ 9-A Video
1-B Catalog	6-A Periodicals	9-B Microfiche
2-A Book Parts	◆ 6-B Newspapers	10-A Search Engines
2-B Contents	◆ 6-C Magazines	10-B Internet
2-C Index	6-D Reader's Guide	10-C Software
2-D Glossary	6-E Vertical Files	◆ 10-D Word Processing
2-E Bibliography	6-F Outside	◆ 10-E Prod. Software
3-A Almanac	7-A Dewey	11-A Organization
3-B Dictionary	◆ 8-A Books	11-B Self-Organization
3-C Thesaurus	◆ 8-B Genres	11-C Topics
3-D Encyclopedia	◆ 8-C Myths	11-D Notes
3-E Record Books	◆ 8-D Tall Tales	11-E Prewrite
4-A Atlas	◆ 8-E Poetry	11-F Outline
4-B Maps	◆ 8-F Awards	11-G Timeline
4-C Gazetteer	◆ 8-G Book Reports	11-H Draft
5-A Biography	8-H Copyright	◆ 11-I Publish

STANDARD 6: THE STUDENT WHO IS AN INDEPENDENT LEARNER IS INFORMATION LITERATE AND *STRIVES* FOR EXCELLENCE IN INFORMATION *SEEKING* AND KNOWLEDGE *GENERATION*.

◆ 1-A Library	◆ 5-B Quotations	◆ 9-A Video
◆ 1-B Catalog	◆ 6-A Periodicals	◆ 9-B Microfiche
◆ 2-A Book Parts	◆ 6-B Newspapers	◆ 10-A Search Engines
◆ 2-B Contents	◆ 6-C Magazines	◆ 10-B Internet
◆ 2-C Index	◆ 6-D Reader's Guide	◆ 10-C Software
◆ 2-D Glossary	◆ 6-E Vertical Files	◆ 10-D Word Processing
◆ 2-E Bibliography	◆ 6-F Outside	◆ 10-E Prod. Software
◆ 3-A Almanac	◆ 7-A Dewey	◆ 11-A Organization
◆ 3-B Dictionary	◆ 8-A Books	◆ 11-B Self-Organization
◆ 3-C Thesaurus	◆ 8-B Genres	◆ 11-C Topics
◆ 3-D Encyclopedia	◆ 8-C Myths	◆ 11-D Notes
◆ 3-E Record Books	◆ 8-D Tall Tales	◆ 11-E Prewrite
◆ 4-A Atlas	◆ 8-E Poetry	◆ 11-F Outline
◆ 4-B Maps	◆ 8-F Awards	◆ 11-G Timeline
◆ 4-C Gazetteer	◆ 8-G Book Reports	◆ 11-H Draft
◆ 5-A Biography	◆ 8-H Copyright	◆ 11-I Publish

Social Responsibility

STANDARD 7: THE STUDENT WHO CONTRIBUTES POSITIVELY TO THE LEARNING COMMUNITY AND TO SOCIETY IS INFORMATION LITERATE AND *RECOGNIZES* THE IMPORTANCE OF INFORMATION TO A DEMOCRATIC SOCIETY.

- ◆ 1-A Library
- ◆ 1-B Catalog
- ◆ 2-A Book Parts
- ◆ 2-B Contents
- ◆ 2-C Index
- ◆ 2-D Glossary
- ◆ 2-E Bibliography
- ◆ 3-A Almanac
- ◆ 3-B Dictionary
- ◆ 3-C Thesaurus
- ◆ 3-D Encyclopedia
- ◆ 3-E Record Books
- ◆ 4-A Atlas
- ◆ 4-B Maps
- ◆ 4-C Gazetteer
- ◆ 5-A Biography

- ◆ 5-B Quotations
- ◆ 6-A Periodicals
- ◆ 6-B Newspapers
- ◆ 6-C Magazines
- ◆ 6-D Reader's Guide
- ◆ 6-E Vertical Files
- ◆ 6-F Outside
- ◆ 7-A Dewey
- ◆ 8-A Books
- ◆ 8-B Genres
- ◆ 8-C Myths
- ◆ 8-D Tall Tales
- ◆ 8-E Poetry
- ◆ 8-F Awards
- ◆ 8-G Book Reports
- ◆ 8-H Copyright

- ◆ 9-A Video
- ◆ 9-B Microfiche
- ◆ 10-A Search Engines
- ◆ 10-B Internet
- ◆ 10-C Software
- ◆ 10-D Word Processing
- ◆ 10-E Prod. Software
- ◆ 11-A Organization
- ◆ 11-B Self-Organization
- ◆ 11-C Topics
- ◆ 11-D Notes
- ◆ 11-E Prewrite
- ◆ 11-F Outline
- ◆ 11-G Timeline
- ◆ 11-H Draft
- ◆ 11-I Publish

STANDARD 8: THE STUDENT WHO CONTRIBUTES POSITIVELY TO THE LEARNING COMMUNITY IS INFORMATION LITERATE AND *PARTICIPATES* EFFECTIVELY IN GROUPS TO PURSUE AND GENERATE INFORMATION.

- ◆ 1-A Library
-    1-B Catalog
-    2-A Book Parts
-    2-B Contents
- ◆ 2-C Index
-    2-D Glossary
-    2-E Bibliography
- ◆ 3-A Almanac
- ◆ 3-B Dictionary
- ◆ 3-C Thesaurus
- ◆ 3-D Encyclopedia
- ◆ 3-E Record Books
-    4-A Atlas
- ◆ 4-B Maps

-    4-C Gazetteer
- ◆ 5-A Biography
-    5-B Quotations
-    6-A Periodicals
- ◆ 6-B Newspapers
-    6-C Magazines
- ◆ 6-D Reader's Guide
-    6-E Vertical Files
-    6-F Outside
- ◆ 7-A Dewey
-    8-A Books
-    8-B Genres
-    8-C Myths
-    8-D Tall Tales

-    8-E Poetry
-    8-F Awards
-    8-G Book Reports
-    8-H Copyright
- ◆ 9-A Video
-    9-B Microfiche
-    10-A Search Engines
-    10-B Internet
-    10-C Software
-    10-D Word Processing
-    10-E Prod. Software
-    11-A Organization
-    11-B Self-Organization
- ◆ 11-C Topics

| 11-D Notes | 11-F Outline | ◆ 11-H Draft |
| 11-E Prewrite | 11-G Timeline | ◆ 11-I Publish |

STANDARD 9: THE STUDENT WHO CONTRIBUTES POSITIVELY TO THE LEARNING COMMUNITY AND TO SOCIETY IS INFORMATION LITERATE AND *PARTICIPATES* EFFECTIVELY IN GROUPS TO PURSUE AND GENERATE INFORMATION.

◆ 1-A Library	5-B Quotations	9-A Video
◆ 1-B Catalog	6-A Periodicals	9-B Microfiche
◆ 2-A Book Parts	◆ 6-B Newspapers	10-A Search Engines
2-B Contents	6-C Magazines	10-B Internet
2-C Index	6-D Reader's Guide	10-C Software
2-D Glossary	6-E Vertical Files	10-D Word Processing
2-E Bibliography	6-F Outside	10-E Prod. Software
◆ 3-A Almanac	◆ 7-A Dewey	11-A Organization
◆ 3-B Dictionary	8-A Books	11-B Self-Organization
◆ 3-C Thesaurus	◆ 8-B Genres	◆ 11-C Topics
◆ 3-D Encyclopedia	◆ 8-C Myths	11-D Notes
3-E Record Books	8-D Tall Tales	11-E Prewrite
◆ 4-A Atlas	8-E Poetry	11-F Outline
◆ 4-B Maps	8-F Awards	11-G Timeline
◆ 4-C Gazetteer	8-G Book Reports	◆ 11-H Draft
◆ 5-A Biography	8-H Copyright	◆ 11-I Publish

Lesson Summary ....

This is an overview of the units, lessons, and rationale for this book. At a glance, the instructor can see the development from the physical plant orientation to the student's own use of the library for finished projects.

Unit 1: Getting to Know Your Library Media Center

A. Mapping the Library Media Center

B. Using the Print and Electronic Card Catalogs

Students need to be familiar with the layout of their library. This unit helps the instructor orient the student. The physical plants of libraries may look different at first, but after learning about the nonfiction, fiction, electronic resources, and reference materials in their library, students should be able to see that using any library is based on the same principles.

Unit 2: Using Reference Resources

A. Learning and Using the Parts of a Reference Book

B. How to Use a Table of Contents

C. How to Use an Index

D. How to Use a Glossary

E. How to Use a Bibliography

After locating reference books, the student needs knowledge of the index, table of contents, and glossary in information gathering. There is a difference between finding a book and finding an answer on your own.

Unit 3: Using Reference Resources: General Information

A. Almanac

B. Dictionary

C. Thesaurus

D. Encyclopedia

E. Record Books

The dictionary, thesaurus, and encyclopedia are the backbone of the reference section of the library. Home libraries usually have a dictionary and thesaurus, but an encyclopedia set that needs to be updated yearly is a large investment. These books are a great place to start looking for general information on a subject or to start topic generation. The dictionary and thesaurus are a part of every word processing program.

Unit 4: Using Reference Resources: Geography

A. Atlas

B. Maps

C. Gazetteer: A Geographical Dictionary

Atlases, maps, and gazetteers, both paper and electronic, answer the question "Where am I?" Although the social studies instructor may develop lessons, there are many times that map reading skills need to be reinforced and used in other areas of the curriculum.

A student should know that maps change and can be found in many different places.

Students should be able to locate the countries and people that make an impact on their daily lives.

Unit 5: Using Reference Resources: Biography and Quotations

A. Biography

B. *Bartlett's Familiar Quotations*

It is important to learn about people. Some people have said and done things that have brought about change or altered history. Finding creditable information to use in research papers is a challenge. Today it is simple to use a magazine or newspaper as the truth. It takes a lot of materials and sources of information to be sure you have an unbiased report.

Unit 6: Using Reference Resources: Current Information

A. Introduction to Periodicals

B. Newspapers

C. Magazines

D. *Reader's Guide to Periodical Literature*

E. Vertical Files

F. Outside the Library Media Center

Everyone should be informed of the current events that have an impact on their lives. Libraries are not the only place to locate information. Students have information all around them if only they would take the time to look. The excuse of "I couldn't get to the library" doesn't mean they couldn't do research. The daily newspaper, the computer, the museum, and yes, even the television can be reference resources.

Unit 7: Dewey Decimal Classification System

A. Dewey Decimal Classification System

Libraries from the school level to major government branches use the classification system to organize and shelf their nonfiction materials. Students must be familiar with the system to find their materials.

Unit 8: Fiction

A. Books from Cover to Cover

B. Student's Literature Genres

C. Folklore, Myths, and Legends

D. Fables, Tall Tales, and Folk Tales

E. Poetry

F. Award Winners

G. Book Reports

H. Copyright

Students use the library for the enjoyment of reading books. This section introduces students to the idea that some books are outstanding and receive awards, and are worthy of special attention. Knowing good literature is important.

The library provides many different genres for many different interests. Students should be directed to quality books. They also should learn how to give credit to the authors of these books and materials. Copyright credit and bibliography information are often overlooked by the students. They tend to use the information as though they were the authors. In today's electronic world, copyright is even more important because of the ease of duplication.

Unit 9: Electronic Materials

A. Videotapes, CDs, DVDs, and Audiotapes

B. Microfiche

Isn't the library mostly paper? The library has come a long way. Electronic forms of books and magazines now occupy shelf space in all libraries. These materials are both good and bad for students. Copyright, faithfulness to novels, ease of duplication, and other issues make electronic materials controversial for student use as reference sources.

Unit 10: Computers and the Internet

A. Search Engines

B. Using the Internet

C. Electronic Reference Software

D. Word Processing

E. Production Software

Who today doesn't know the value of computers and the Internet? Few are able to do anything that is not affected by a computer.

The production of a professional-looking product to show the information a student has gathered is often assisted by word processing software and the Internet. It isn't enough to gather information. Students should produce a paper or project that shows they really can organize and use the information for a purpose.

Unit 11: Using What You Have Learned: Writing and Publishing

A. Organizational Systems

B. Self-Organization

C. Topic Generation

D. Note Taking

E. Prewriting

F. Basic Outlining

G. Timeline

H. Draft Writing

I. Publishing

The number one goal of the library is to develop students who can use the library effectively. Students should be able to use the library for entertainment and information. They will evaluate the available materials and choose the best resources for their projects. Teachers want students who can produce a finished product that shows mastery of research and understanding.

How to Use This Book . . . .

As shown in the preceding lesson summary, *Media Center Discovery* is divided into eleven different units, each of which contains one or more lessons. Each lesson begins with a lesson description page that is followed by one or more of four types of activities: transparencies, activities, worksheets, and games. The transparencies can be copied for display on an overhead projector. The worksheets can be copied and handed out to the students to complete (answers to the worksheets appear at the end of the lesson description page). And activities and games can be led by the librarian or instructor.

Each type of activity is numbered consecutively within the unit in which it appears (Worksheet 3.1, Worksheet 3.2, Transparency 3.1, Transparency 3.2, and so on). In other words, there may be a Worksheet 3.2 and a Transparency 3.2 within the same unit (Unit 3 in this case), although not necessarily within the same lesson. The table of contents provides a guide, as does each lesson description page, and each activity is clearly marked with the title, designation, number, and identifying icon.

Getting the Most Out of Your Library

1. Explore the layout of your library media center

2. Understand the organizational systems of your library media center

3. Learn how to locate materials with the card catalog

4. Become familiar with the computer catalog

5. Search for fiction and nonfiction books and information

6. Locate audio- and videotapes, vertical file—pictures, maps, and so on

7. Apply available reference materials in research projects

8. Find magazines and periodicals using the readers' guide

9. Understand and use the parts of books

10. Evaluate what you find

   A. Judge the accuracy

   B. Consider the source

   C. Compare more than one source

 TRANSPARENCY 0.1

Library Media Center Organizational Systems

FICTION

Alphabetical

Author's last name

Title (A, An, The)

Subject

Numerical

Chronological

Historical fiction

Subject

Alphabetical

NONFICTION

Alphabetical

Author's last name

Title (A, An, The)

Subject

Numerical

Dewey Decimal classification

Chronological

Historical sequence

Subject

Alphabetical

REFERENCE

Alphabetical

Title (A, An, The)

Subject

Material (almanac, atlas, and so on)

Numerical

Dewey Decimal classification

Chronological

Historical sequence

Subject

Alphabetical

BIOGRAPHY

Alphabetical

Title (A, An, The)

Person—Last name, first name

Numerical

92—Biography

920—Group biography

Chronological

Time sequence

Subject

Alphabetical

 **TRANSPARENCY 0.2**

Sample Reference Materials

Reference books are reliable sources because the information has been written and checked by experts, and organized in alphabetical order, by subject, by date, or by geographical region.

Type of Reference	Kind of Information	Examples
Encyclopedia	General information articles; variety of topics	*World Book*
Dictionary	Spellings and definitions of words	*Webster's*
Atlas	Maps and geographical information	*World Atlas*
Almanac	Facts and statistics	*Information Please Almanac*
Thesaurus	Synonyms for commonly used words	*Roget's*

Three Important Parts of Reference Books and Nonfiction Books

Copyright date: gives the year the book was published; current information

Table of contents: lists chapter titles and page numbers

Index: lists important topics and details covered in the book; specific details about topic

TRANSPARENCY 0.3

Questions

1. **What is important about having current information?**
   Everyone needs to know the latest information in all areas of reference.

2. **Why do you look at the table of contents or index of a reference book?**
   Looking at the table of contents or index speeds up the location of subjects and topics.

3. **Where would you find the index of an encyclopedia?**
   The last volume of an encyclopedia set is the index volume.

4. **Which reference book would you choose to learn about the rivers in Colorado?**
   The atlas provides geography information.

5. **Which reference book would you choose to learn the definition of "natatorium"?**
   The dictionary provides word definitions.

6. **Which reference book would you choose to learn another word for "directory"?**
   The thesaurus provides alternative words for the same thing.

7. **Which reference book would you choose to learn general information about television?**
   The encyclopedia provides general information about various topics.

8. **Which reference book would you choose to find out who won the 2002 Super Bowl?**
   An almanac provides information about current or recent events.

TRANSPARENCY 0.4

About the Author

....

BARBARA R. HAMM has taught in both public and parochial schools for over twenty-six years. She has been a classroom teacher, a computer specialist, and a library media specialist.

She is a graduate of Harris Teachers College with a bachelor of science degree, specializing in elementary education. She received her master of education degree from the University of Missouri-St. Louis in instructional media technology, and she received her library certification from the University of Missouri-Columbia. Her professional credentials also include a life certificate in elementary education and certifications as a learning resources director, library media specialist, and instructional designer.

Hamm received the MO-CAPE Educator or Achievement Award and the Emerson Electric Excellence in Teaching Award in 1996. She is also listed in *Who's Who Among America's Teachers 1994*, the "Best Teachers in America Selected by the Best Students."

Her first book, *Let's Discover Computers,* is used by educators to teach students from kindergarten through grade 3 the basics of computers through storytelling, activities, and games.

As a library media specialist, Hamm developed curriculums for library and computer education. She has also developed many strategies to help her students locate research materials in the school library media center as well as in public libraries.

UNIT
ONE

Getting to Know Your
Library Media Center

LESSON 1-A

....

Mapping the Library Media Center

To the Instructor ....

How many times a day do students ask, "Where can I find …?" or "Where is …?" One way to develop independent learners at every grade level is to spend time at the beginning of each school year reviewing the arrangement of materials in your library media center.

Objectives ....

1. Students become familiar with the library media center by completing outline maps or by creating their own maps of the library.

2. Students understand where to locate various source materials in the library.

Materials ....

Transparencies

1.1 Library Media Center Floor Plan □ ◨ ■

1.2 Dewey Decimal Classification List ◨ ■

Transparency of your library floor plan (no page) □ ◨ ■

Representative materials from the library shelves

Teaching and Preparation . . . .

1. Conduct a tour of the library media center.

2. Use a transparency to review the organization of your library resources. Modify the transparency to meet your needs.

3. Introduce the types of materials in your library.

4. Review the various tasks that would be carried out at the circulation desk and search stations.

5. Have students complete maps and other activities.

6. Review Internet references

   http://lii.org (Librarians Index to the Internet)

   http://www.loc.gov (Library of Congress)

   http://www.ipl.org (Internet Public Library)

   http://www.xrefer.com

   http://www.ed.gov/ (Department of Education)

Activities . . . .

1.1 Library Map Labels ☐ ◨

1.2 Create an Outline Map ◨ ■

1.3 Location, Location, Location (Note: Crossword puzzle was made with the use of http://www.puzzlemaker.com.) ☐ ◨

Students map the library media center on their own. Variation: students design their own library media center. (no page) ◨ ■

Compare Dewey Classification sections with sections in your library. (no page) ◨ ■

Worksheets . . . .

1.1 Scavenger Hunt ☐ ◨ ■

1.2 Location, Location ◨ ■

1.3 Fiction/Nonfiction Order ◨ ■

1.4 Titles to Locate ◨ ■

1.5 Where Can I Find It? ☐ ◨ ■

Games ....

1.1 Plant a Flag ☐ ◨

1.2 Team Plant a Flag ◨ ◼

1.3 Plant a Flag—Individuals ☐ ◨ ◼

1.4 Trivia Research ◨ ◼

Connections to the Curriculum ....

Locate the sections of the library where you will find the following:

Art—artist biographies

Language arts—spelling word list—dictionary

Math—math games—Dewey section 510

Music—recording of Mozart—audio collection

Physical education—athletic records—Dewey section 030

Science—*National Geographic* article about ants—periodicals

Social studies—video of prehistoric animals—video collection

Answer Key ....

ACTIVITY 1.4

Crossword puzzle answers appear on the page following the puzzle.

WORKSHEET 1.1

1. Dictionary
2. Card catalog
3. Almanac
4. Dewey/Encyclopedia
5. Biography
6. Thesaurus
7. Encyclopedia
8. Dictionary
9. Newspaper
10. Atlas

WORKSHEET 1.2

Location answers will vary.

1. Circulation desk
2. Card catalog
3. Paperbacks section
4. Card catalog
5. Reference section
6. Biography section
7. Dictionary
8. Computer
9. Newspapers
10. New acquisitions section

WORKSHEET 1.3

Fiction

1. F/ADA
2. F/ALC
3. F/BIA
4. F/CLE
5. F/CLE
6. F/FAR
7. F/GIP
8. F/LIT
9. F/SAC
10. F/SPY

Nonfiction

1. 385/DAY
2. 387/HOA
3. 568/DAL
4. 636.6/ZIM
5. 636.7/POS
6. 636.8/FED
7. 793.7/AND
8. 796.6/EVA
9. 796.7/RAD
10. 798.2/GRE

WORKSHEET 1.4

1. Nonfiction
2. Reference
3. Fiction
4. Reference
5. Fiction
6. Nonfiction
7. Reference
8. Fiction
9. Nonfiction
(10). Answers 6 and 9

WORKSHEET 1.5

1. d
2. f
3. c
4. e
5. c
6. b
7. e
8. a
9. h
10. b
11. b
12. g

GAME 1.1

1. Periodicals
2. Reference
3. Circulation desk
4. Electronic materials
5. Electronic materials
6. Periodicals
7. Computer area
8. Biography section
9. Reference—atlas
10. Dewey—900s

Library Media Center Floor Plan

Circulation desk	Internet computers
Reference shelf	Word processing computers
Biography	Videotapes
Fiction	Audiotapes
Nonfiction	Dictionary stand
Newspapers	Television
Periodicals	Book truck
Vertical file	Display case
Paperback display	New acquisitions

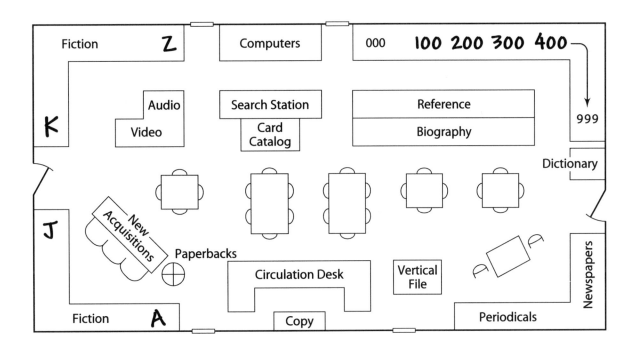

TRANSPARENCY 1.1

Dewey Decimal Classification List

010	Bibliography		510	Mathematics
020	Library Science		520	Astronomy
030	General Encyclopedias		530	Physics
040	General Collected Essays		540	Chemistry and Allied Sciences
050	General Periodicals		550	Earth Sciences
060	General Societies		560	Paleontology
070	Newspaper Journalism		570	Anthropology and Biology
080	Collected Works		580	Botanical Sciences
090	Manuscript and Rare Books		590	Zoological Sciences
110	Metaphysics		610	Medical Sciences
120	Metaphysical Theories		620	Engineering
130	Branches of Psychology		630	Agriculture
140	Philosophical Topics		640	Home Economics
150	General Psychology		650	Business
160	Logic		660	Chemical Technology
170	Ethics		670	Manufactures
180	Ancient and Medieval		680	Other Manufactures
190	Modern Philosophy		690	Building Construction
210	Natural Theology		710	Landscape and Civil Art
220	Bible		720	Architecture
230	Doctrinal Theology		730	Sculpture
240	Devotional and Practical		740	Drawing and Decorative Arts
250	Pastoral Theology		750	Painting
260	Christian Church		760	Prints and Print Making
270	Christian Church History		770	Photography
280	Christian Churches and Sects		780	Music
290	Other Religions		790	Recreation
310	Statistics		810	American Literature in English
320	Political Science		820	English and Old English
330	Economics		830	Germanic Literatures
340	Law		840	French, Provencal, Catalan
350	Public Administration		850	Italian and Rumanian
360	Social Welfare		860	Spanish and Portuguese
370	Education		870	Latin and Other Italic Literature
380	Public Services and Utilities		880	Classical and Modern Greek
390	Customs and Folklore		890	Other Literature
410	Comparative Linguistics		910	Geography, Travels, Description
420	English and Anglo-Saxon		920	Biography
430	Germanic Languages		930	Ancient History
440	French, Provencal, Catalan		940	Europe
450	Italian and Rumanian		950	Asia
460	Spanish and Portuguese		960	Africa
470	Latin and Other Italic		970	North America
480	Classical and Modern Greek		980	South America
490	Other Languages		990	Other Parts of the World

TRANSPARENCY 1.2

Library Map Labels

Directions: Students receive copies of this page and write their names in each section, then cut this page apart. Students will place each section in the correct area of the library media center. The teacher, the librarian, or peers may then collect the labels, or they can be collected by another class. There can be a game or activity to check for the accuracy. The idea is for students to check and help each other locate the materials.

Fiction	Circulation Desk
Nonfiction	Copy Machine
Reference (circulating)	Card Catalog (print)
Reference (noncirculating)	Card Catalog (electronic)
Periodicals	New Acquisitions
Picture Books	Audio
Paperbacks	Visual
Vertical Files	Word Processors

Create an Outline Map

Directions: Students draw the floor plan of your library media center (including windows, doors, and so on). In the Location column, write directions such as "Northeast corner." Students can then compare floor plans to check for accuracy.

Resource	Location
Audiotapes	
Biography	
Card catalog	
CD-ROM, computer software	
Circulation desk	
Copy machine	
Dictionary stand	
Display cases	
Internet search computers	
Periodicals: newspapers, magazines	
Paperback books	
Reference shelves	
Tables and chairs	
Television	
Vertical file	
Videotapes	

Location, Location, Location

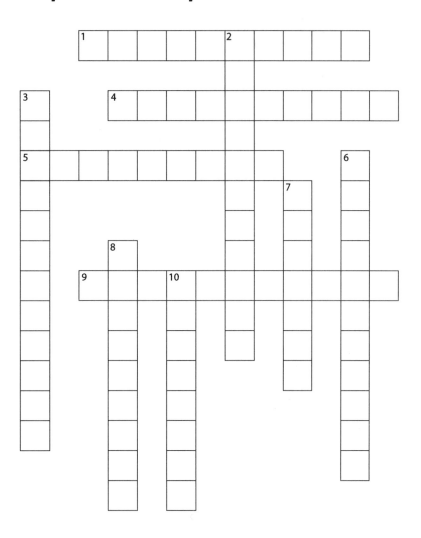

Across

1. Real information

4. Books printed with soft covers

5. Materials used only in the library

9. Desk where books are borrowed and returned

Down

2. Search for books available in the library

3. Storage of large maps and pictures

6. Newspapers and magazines

7. Make-believe stories

8. Books about a person's life

10. Equipment used to access the Internet or do word processing

Location, Location, Location
Crossword Solution

```
          ¹N  O  N  F  I  ²C  T  I  O  N
                          A
    ³V          ⁴P  A  P  E  R  B  A  C  K  S
    E                     D
    R  E  F  E  R  E  N  C  E          ⁶P
    T                     A      ⁷F      E
    I                     T      I       R
    C          ⁸B         A      C       I
    A       ⁹C  I  R ¹⁰C  U  L  A  T  I  O  N
    L          O     O    L      I       D
    F          G     M    O      O       I
    I          R     P    G      N       C
    L          A     U                   A
    E          P     T                   L
               H     E                   S
               Y     R
```

Across

1. Real information

4. Books printed with soft covers

5. Materials used only in the library

9. Desk where books are borrowed and returned

Down

2. Place to search for books available in the library

3. Storage of large maps and pictures

6. Newspapers and magazines

7. Make-believe stories

8. Book about a person's life

10. Equipment used to access the Internet or do word processing

NAME _____   DATE _____

Scavenger Hunt

What do I **need**? Where do I **go** to discover the **answer**? (Use with library map)

1. Where can I check the way a word is spelled?

2. Where can I find out if the library has a book about computers?

3. Where would I go to learn which baseball team won the World Series in 1990?

4. Where can I find information about what food parakeets eat?

5. Where would I go to find out how many home runs Babe Ruth hit in his career?

6. Where can I go to find out if there is another word to use in place of the word *help*?

7. Where could I find what general information is available about butterflies?

8. Where would I learn how to pronounce a word?

9. Where can I find the weather forecast for tomorrow?

10. Where can I find how far it is from the city where I live to the capital city of my state?

Location, Location

Directions: You are always asking the librarian to help you find materials. Today you will give the directions. The answers will supply directions and name the section of the library. Answers will include "north," "south," "east," or "west," or "right" or "left," like a treasure map.

Example: We will watch a video about using the library. Go to the <u>television activity area</u>. It's located <u>on the north wall</u>.

1. To return your borrowed books you go to the _____. It's located on the _____ wall.

2. To locate a fiction book for a book report you go to the _____. It is located _____.

3. You want to borrow a paperback version of the book. It is located

   _____.

4. You want to find out if the library has a book about insects. You will use the

   _____. It is located _____.

5. The reference books are located _____.

6. Your social studies teacher wants you to learn about the life of Abraham Lincoln. You go

   to the _____.

7. You need to learn at least three definitions for the word *idea.* You will use the

   _____ located _____.

8. You need to do research using the Internet. You will use the _____

   located _____.

9. You need to find the top news story of the day. You will use the

   _____ located _____.

10. The librarian has announced the arrival of some new books on penguins. You will go

    to the _____ located _____.

NAME _____   DATE _____

Fiction/Nonfiction Order

Directions: Use the card catalog information to place these titles in alphabetical order, with the fiction books in one column and the nonfiction books in the second column according to their spine-level information.

F CLE	Beverly Cleary *Henry and Beezus*	568 DAL	Kathleen Daly *Dinosaurs*	F ADA	Richard Adams *Watership Down*
636.6 ZIM	Herbert S. Zim *Parakeets*	F FAR	Walter Farley *The Black Stallion*	385 DAY	John Day *Trains*
F BIA	Elsa Biak *Tizz and Company*	387 HOA	Robert Hoare *Travel by Sea*	F LIT	Jean Little *From Anna*
796.7 RAD	Edward Radlauer *Wild Wheels*	F CLE	Beverly Cleary *Henry Huggins*	796.6 EVA	Ken Evans *Cycling*
F ALC	Louisa M. Alcott *Little Women*	636.8 FED	Jan Feder *Life of a Cat*	F GIP	Fred Gipson *Old Yeller*
798.2 GRE	Carol Green *Let's Ride*	F SPY	Johanna Spyri *Heidi*	793.7 AND	V. Anderson *Thinking Games Book*
F SAC	Marilyn Sachs *Bus Ride*	636.7 POS	Elsa Posell *Dogs*		

Place the information above into either of the two columns, Fiction or Nonfiction. Be sure to write the spine label, author, and title in the correct order.

Fiction

Spine label	Author	Title
1.		
2.		
3.		
4.		
5.		
6.		
7.		
8.		
9.		
10.		

Nonfiction

Spine label	Author	Title
1.		
2.		
3.		
4.		
5.		
6.		
7.		
8.		
9.		
10.		

NAME _____ DATE _____

Titles to Locate

Locate materials by using your knowledge of the three main sections of the library: **fiction,** stories and novels created from the author's imagination, arranged alphabetically by the author's last name; **nonfiction,** factual information about many subjects arranged by classification numbers and then the author's last name, and biographical and autobiographical books arranged by the subject's last name; and **reference,** including encyclopedias, dictionaries, atlases, almanacs, newspapers, magazines, and the *Reader's Guide to Periodical Literature.*

Directions: Write "fiction," "nonfiction," or "reference" to tell where you would find the following materials.

1. *The Story of My Life* by Helen Keller   _____

2. *USA Today*   _____

3. *Charlotte's Web* by E. B. White   _____

4. *The World Almanac*   _____

5. *The Call of the Wild* by Jack London   _____

6. *Pet Care for Beginners*   _____

7. *National Geographic* magazine   _____

8. *My Side of the Mountain* by Betsy Byars   _____

9. *Fodor's Europe*   _____

Which of these materials would be found using a combination of the classification number and the author's last name? (write the material's numbers)

NAME _____ DATE _____

Where Can I Find It?

Directions: Match the items in Column 1 with the correct section in Column 2. Write the letter on the line. Some letters may be used more than once.

Column 1

____ 1. *Cricket Magazine*

____ 2. *World Book,* volume P

____ 3. *The Greatest: Muhammad Ali* by Walter Dean Myers

____ 4. *Jumanji* by Chris Ahlsburg

____ 5. *Rosa Parks: My Story* by Rosa Parks

____ 6. *Scholastic Children's Thesaurus*

____ 7. *Mary McLeod Bethune* by Eloise Greenfield

____ 8. *Amphibians in Danger* by Ron Fridell

____ 9. *American Tall Tales* by Mary Pope Osborne

____ 10. *World Almanac*

____ 11. *Scholastic Dictionary of Idioms*

____ 12. *A Dinosaur Named Sue* by Patricia Relf

Column 2

a. Nonfiction animals

b. Reference

c. Biography

d. Periodicals

e. Fiction A–J

f. Encyclopedias

g. Fiction K–Z

h. Nonfiction folk tales and legends

GAME 1.1

Plant a Flag

Directions: Answer the question by planting a flag (card with your team name) with the resource that will answer each question. One member of the team writes the results of your team's search in the space below the question. Be the first team to answer all the questions correctly!

Where would you locate . . .

1. A magazine about animals?

2. A dictionary with more than one thousand pages?

3. The place to check in or out a book?

4. An audio recording of a book?

5. A video of a book?

6. A newspaper?

7. An Internet computer?

8. A biography of President George Washington?

9. A book of maps?

10. A book about the state where you live?

18

Copyright © 2004 John Wiley and Sons, Inc.

Team Plant a Flag

Directions: Cut columns apart. Place in a box. The team captain chooses the list his or her team will research. The captain will use color-coded flags for his or her team and place a flag with the corresponding number in the volume or location indication. Number one on the list must have the number one flag, and so on. The winning team is the one that completes the list, placing the correct flags in the correct places in the shortest amount of time.

A	B	C	D
1. Encyclopedia Q	1. Map of Japan	1. Children's dictionary page for letter Z	1. Life of Abraham Lincoln
2. Magazine about sports	2. Newspaper sports page	2. Check out a book	2. Map of Israel
3. Map of Australia	3. Children's dictionary page for letter X	3. Magazine for girls	3. Year Alaska became a state
4. Biographical dictionary	4. Check in a book	4. Life of George Washington	4. Computer
5. Life of Paul Revere	5. Encyclopedia X	5. Year Arizona became a state	5. Newspaper headline
6. Newspaper comics	6. Year Maine became a state	6. Computer	6. Children's dictionary page for letter I
7. Check in a book	7. Computer	7. Encyclopedia Z	7. Biographical dictionary
8. Year Hawaii became a state	8. Magazine for boys	8. Biographical dictionary	8. Check out a book
9. Computer	9. Biographical dictionary	9. Newspaper front page	9. Magazine about nature
10. Children's dictionary	10. Life of Christopher Columbus	10. Map of Brazil	10. Encyclopedia I

Plant a Flag–Individuals

Directions: Continue the game by being the first to write a fact you discovered in each of the following reference materials:

Write the title and one fact.

1. Dictionary

2. Atlas

3. Almanac

4. Newspaper

5. *Guinness Book of Records*

6. Thesaurus

7. Other interesting book

I like the _____ best because _____

_____

Trivia Research

To the Instructor

Students can play this game after they have been instructed and had practice using several different reference books.

Objectives

1. Students will use the card catalog or electronic card catalog to locate information.

2. Students will use reference books to answer questions prepared by the librarian or collaborating subject teachers.

3. Students will work together as a team using each other's strengths.

4. * *Variation:* Students will use the Internet computers to search for correct answers.

Materials

Questions on 3 x 5 inch cards for students to discover the key words and search using reference books. Be sure the correct answers are written on a separate sheet with corresponding numbers for quick verification of correctness.
Reference books
* Internet computers

Activities

The librarian divides the class into teams of three or four.

Students choose from the stack of prepared questions.

Students use the card catalog and reference books to locate information.

Students write answers on a recording sheet.

* This may be ongoing over several weeks or one class period.

The winners are the teams with the most correct answers.

Reward team winners with recognition on a bulletin board with medals or stickers, or in the school newspaper.

Connections to the Curriculum

Subject teachers can contribute questions for the game.

LESSON 1-B

Using the Print and Electronic Card Catalogs

To the Instructor ....

The print and electronic databases are compared.

Objectives ....

1. Students learn that all items in the library may be located using author, title, subject, or key word information.

2. Students learn how to use the paper and electronic catalogs (databases) to gather information and complete a call slip or printout about the resource, and then to retrieve the materials using the call slip or printout.

Materials ....

Transparencies

1.3 Card Catalog Glossary ☐ ◩ ■

1.4 Electronic Catalog Search ☐ ◩ ■

1.5 How to Use the Online Catalog ☐ ◩ ■

Transparency of electronic card catalog printout (no page) ▯■ ■

Sample card catalog cards
Computer with electronic card catalog access
Printouts from electronic card catalog

Teaching and Preparation . . . .

1. Use the transparencies to demonstrate how to locate materials.

2. Use Transparency 1.4 to show how to locate materials by using the electronic catalog.

3. Use a sample call slip and printout from the electronic catalog and demonstrate how to locate these materials in the library media center.

Activities . . . .

1.4 Creating Catalog Cards □ ▯■ ■

1.5 Call Slip to Material Retrieval □ ▯■ ■

1.6 Look It Up ▯■ ■

Review actual author, title, and subject catalog cards. Use old or extra cards for practice. (no page) □ ▯■ ■

Arrange fiction cards into groups by author, title, and subject. Use old or extra cards for practice. (no page) □ ▯■ ■

Create a card catalog set for a pretend book the student has written. Students file cards in the correct order when completed. (no page) □ ▯■ ■

Worksheets . . . .

1.6 Identify the Parts of a Card □ ▯■ ■

1.7 Identify the Information on a Card □ ▯■

1.8 Catalog to Spine Label ▯■ ■

1.9 Practice Electronic Search □ ▯■ ■

1.10 Research Skills □ ▯■

1.11 Which Is Best? ▯■ ■

1.12 Match Author, Subject, and Title ▯■ ■

Game ....

1.5 Pass the Torch (Tic-Tac-Toe) □ ◨ ■

Connections to the Curriculum ....

Research project: Travel by boat

Art—locate pictures of paintings with naval backgrounds

Language arts—write a newsletter about traveling by boats

Math—research the costs of cruises

Science—research about hurricane season

Social studies—view travel videos to select destination

Answer Key ....

ACTIVITIES 1.4, 1.5, AND 1.6

Answers will vary.

WORKSHEET 1.6

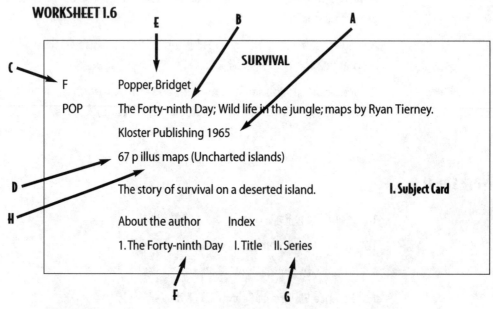

WORKSHEET 1.7

1. 372.3/HAM   5. Barbara R. Hamm   8. A
2. B   6. C   9. False
3. HAM   7. Computers   10. True
4. *Let's Discover Computers*

WORKSHEET 1.8

1. F/ADA
2. F/ALC
3. 793.7/AND
4. F/BIA
5. F/CLE
6. F/CLE
7. 568/DAL
8. 385/DAY
9. 796.6/EVA
10. F/FAR
11. 636.8/FED
12. F/GIP
13. 798.2/GRE
14. 387/HOA
15. F/LIT
16. 636.7/POS
17. 796.7/RAD
18. F/SAC
19. F/SPY
20. 636.6/ZIM

WORKSHEET 1.9

Answers will vary.

WORKSHEET 1.10

1. Print or electronic catalog (database)
2. a. Author
   b. Title
   c. Subject
   d. Key word
3. Last name alphabetically
4. Alphabetically
5. Nonfiction
6. To remember the information retrieved
7. Answers will vary.

WORKSHEET 1.11

1. Copperheads
2. Nonfiction fact book
3. Verdi
4. The information says PICTUREBK.
5. The call number is 793.7HAL. It will be in the nonfiction 700s.

WORKSHEET 1.12

9 numbers
3 school
10 fairy tales
2 holidays
1 monkeys
8 wizards
5 river adventure
6 poetry
4 art
7 winter
11 biography

8 *The Sorcerer's Stone*
5 *Tom Sawyer* and *Huckleberry Finn*
1 *Curious George Visits the Zoo*
6 *The New Kid on the Block*
4 *The Great Thumbprint Drawing*
11 *Abraham Lincoln*
3 *Miss Nelson Is Missing*
9 *Anno's Counting Book*
10 *Snow White*
7 *The Snowman*
2 *Arthur's Thanksgiving*

Card Catalog Glossary

Author   The person or persons who wrote the book. A joint author, illustrator, editor, or compiler might be listed.

Author card   The catalog card with the author's name as the first information seen. The name is printed last name comma first name.

Call number   The information in the upper left-hand corner of a catalog card, seen on the spine label of library material. The call reference number includes the Dewey number if non-fiction, the B for biography, F/Fic for fiction, or REF for reference. The call number will include the first three letters of the author's last name, or the person a biography is about.

Card catalog   The database of the library media center.

Catalog cards   Paper cards in a series of wooden box drawers organized by author, title, and subject.

Main entry card   The base card from which all the others are made. For most books, the main entry base card is an author card.

Copyright date   The year a book is published and the exclusive rights to print the material.

Narrative   A selection of information for research. Sometimes the word *story* is used in a narrative.

Publisher   The company who produced the book and the city where it was printed.

Series   Titles that have several separate volumes as part of a set. Some series might be found in the reference section.

Subject card   The catalog card with the topic of the book listed first on the catalog card.

Title   The name of a book. Sometimes the subtitle may have a card. The articles *A, An,* and *The* are ignored when alphabetizing the title of the book.

Tracings   Additional cards that have a subject heading and are ones that will provide the assistance and additional information about the materials.

Electronic Catalog Search

Similarities in all electronic searches.

1. Easy to use.

2. Provide printable, take-along information.

3. Give fast results.

Search Screen Information

To Search

1. Click on the hypertext word of author, title, or subject.

   Search Questions

   > **Author:** Are the author's names typed in *last* name first or *first* name first?

   > **Title:** Do you type *A, An,* or *The* if the title begins with these words? Does it make a difference to the search if you do not?

   > **Subject:** Is spelling important?

   > **Word:** Is spelling important?

   > **Call Number (Dewey):** Do you know the classification numbers?

2. Click on Help Information. What are the items covered by the help screen? (Answers will vary.)

3. Click on Interlibrary Loan. What are the steps to acquire materials from another library? (Answers will vary.)

4. View Personal Information. Are you required to give personal information to check out a book?

5. E-mail notification.

6. Request items the library should acquire.

 **TRANSPARENCY 1.4**

How to Use the Online Catalog

Searches may be done in the paper catalog or the electronic catalog. There are advantages to both.

Search display screens are made to be helpful to everyone.

Author Search

Search for authors, composers, music groups, cast members, editors, illustrators, government entities, or organizations

- Type the author's *last name* first.
- You may also type the name of an organization or governmental body.

Examples

> Twain, Mark
> Rams

Author/Title Search

If you are unsure of an exact title but you know the author's last name and a word from the title

- Type the author's *last name* in the author box
- Type a word or words from the title

Examples

> Twain, Mark

> Huckleberry

Title Search

Use if you know the whole title or the beginning of the title. If you only know a word from the title, you might want to try an Author/title search or a Word search.

Examples

> Happy House on High Hill

Subject Search

- Type in the subject you're interested in and then click "Submit Search."

Call Number Search

Use if you already know the call number you're looking for

- Type and expand a call number search by shortening the call number. Be sure to include all punctuation (i.e. "/","",".").

Note that if you shorten the call number, such as to 398.2, the computer will retrieve every call number that begins with those numbers and allow you to browse the list.

Word Search

- Type the words you want

   Adjacency: Multiple words are searched together as one phrase. (Examples: George Washington, World War II, London England, Fraternal order of)

   Truncation: Words may be right-hand truncated using an asterisk * to truncate from one to five characters. Use a double asterisk ** for open-ended truncation. The results of such searches usually give too many hits to be effective. (Examples: hydro* results in over three million hits; hydro** results in over five million hits.)

   Operators: Use "and" or "or" to specify multiple words in any field, any order. Use "and not" to exclude words. Parentheses group words together when using Boolean operators. (Examples: George and Martha Washington, John Adams or John Quincy Adams, George Bush not George W. Bush)

   Proximity: Use "near" to specify words close to each other, in any order. Use "within #" to specify terms which occur within # words of each other in the record. (Examples: World War I, World War II; John Adams, John Quincy Adams)

   Fields: Specify fields to search, using field abbreviation. Fields available for this database are a: (author), t: (title), s: (subject), and n: (note.) Fields are usually used in library author and/or book searches.

The search displays will vary according to whether or not your search was general or specific, or whether words were spelled correctly. The display will show all items that exactly matched the search criteria listed. From this display you can begin a new search or limit the search by date, media, or location. Click on the highlighted test of the selection that best matches the search.

A definite advantage of electronic catalogs is that a patron can request items easily—just click the "request" button and fill out the information. In a public library system the patron would designate the branch library to pick up the materials.

TRANSPARENCY 1.5 cont.

Creating Catalog Cards

Directions: Students will pretend they have written a book, either fiction or nonfiction. They can then do the following:

1. Make the three cards for a card catalog set (subject, author, title) about the book. If the book is nonfiction, use the correct Dewey Classification number for the call number.

2. Make up an ISBN number.

3. File the cards in correct order in a pretend card catalog.

4. Write a short summary of the book.

5. Write a short paragraph "about the author."

_____

_____

_____   _____

_____   _____

           p.cm.

           ISBN: _____

_____

_____

_____

_____

_____   _____

_____   _____

           p.cm.

           ISBN: _____

_____

_____

_____

_____

_____

_____

_____

p.cm.

ISBN: _____

_____

_____

Call Slip to Material Retrieval

Use call slips to write information obtained from the print or electronic card catalogs. Search sheet lists are used to mix the searches. Both fiction and nonfiction books and materials should be located.

Call Slip

Call Number _____

First three letters of last name of author _____

    Full name of author (last name first) _____

    Title _____

Search Sheet

Call Number	Author (last, first)	Title

Variations

Provide students with a list of materials to locate. Have the students produce a printout for each item from the electronic catalog. Then have the students locate and retrieve each item on their list.

Look It Up

Directions: Students go to the library and locate a book on each of the subjects listed. The books can be fiction or nonfiction. They should write the title, author, and an F or N for whether the book is fiction or nonfiction, and should choose one to read.

Fairy tale

Title: _____

Author: _____

Fiction or nonfiction _____

Knights or castles

Title: _____

Author: _____

Fiction or nonfiction _____

Civil War

Title: _____

Author: _____

Fiction or nonfiction _____

Famous person

Title: _____

Author: _____

Fiction or nonfiction _____

Dinosaurs

Title: _____

Author: _____

Fiction or nonfiction _____

Travel

Title: _____

Author: _____

Fiction or nonfiction _____

Old West

Title: _____

Author: _____

Fiction or nonfiction _____

Myth

Title: _____

Author: _____

Fiction or Nonfiction _____

Alternatives

Students can choose other time periods, wars, and so on that they are studying in classes. After they are comfortable with using their searching skills, they will be able to locate any book quickly.

Identify the Parts of a Card

Directions: Identify the parts of a card by writing "A,""B,""C," and so on from the list below next to the corresponding part in the card illustration.

SURVIVAL

F   Popper, Bridget

POP The Forty-ninth Day; Wild life in the jungle; maps by Ryan Tierney.

    Kloster Publishing 1965

    67 p illus maps (Uncharted islands)

    The story of survival on a deserted island.

    About the author Index

    1. The Forty-ninth Day I. Title II. Series

A. Copyright date

B. Title

C. Call number

D. Number of pages

E. Author

F. Tracings

G. Series

H. Visual aids

I. Type of card:

NAME   DATE

Identify the Information
on a Card

372.3	Hamm, Barbara R.	
HAM	Let's Discover Computers	
	p. cm.	
	ISBN 0-87928-271-0 (paper)—ISBN 0-87628-520-5 (spiral)	A
	1. Computers—Juvenile literature. I. Title	
QA76.23H35 1997		

Let's Discover Computers

372.3	Hamm, Barbara R.	
HAM	Let's Discover Computers	
	p. cm.	
	ISBN 0-87928-271-0 (paper)—ISBN 0-87628-520-5 (spiral)	B
	1. Computers—Juvenile literature. I. Title	
QA76.23H35 1997		

COMPUTERS

372.3	Hamm, Barbara R.	
HAM	Let's Discover Computers	
	p. cm.	
	ISBN 0-87928-271-0 (paper)—ISBN 0-87628-520-5 (spiral)	C
	1. Computers—Juvenile literature. I. Title	
QA76.23H35 1997		

NAME _____ DATE _____

Directions: Use the sample catalog cards to answer the following questions by filling in the blank space with the correct response.

1. The call number is

2. The title card is letter

3. The author's name as it appears on the spine label is

4. The title is

5. The author's name is

6. The subject card is letter

7. The subject of the book is

8. The author card is letter

9. This is a fiction book. (true or false)

10. There are two different forms of this book. (true or false)

NAME _____   DATE _____

Catalog to Spine Label

Directions: Here is information that you would see on a card catalog card. Use the information to place the books in alphabetical order by spine label.

F CLE	Beverly Cleary *Henry and Beezus*		568 DAL	Kathleen Daly *Dinosaurs*		F ADA	Richard Adams *Watership Down*
636.6 ZIM	Herbert S. Zim *Parakeets*		F FAR	Walter Farley *The Black Stallion*		385 DAY	John Day *Trains*
F BIA	Elsa Biak *Tizz and Company*		387 HOA	Robert Hoare *Travel by Sea*		F LIT	Jean Little *From Anna*
796.7 RAD	Edward Radlauer *Wild Wheels*		F CLE	Beverly Cleary *Henry Huggins*		796.6 EVA	Ken Evans *Cycling*
F ALC	Louisa M. Alcott *Little Women*		636.8 FED	Jan Feder *Life of a Cat*		F GIP	Fred Gipson *Old Yeller*
798.2 GRE	Carol Green *Let's Ride*		F SPY	Johanna Spyri *Heidi*		793.7 AND	V. Anderson *Thinking Games Book*
F SAC	Marilyn Sachs *Bus Ride*		636.7 POS	Elsa Posell *Dogs*			

Place these books in alphabetical card catalog order

	Spine label	Author	Title
1.			
2.			
3.			
4.			
5.			
6.			
7.			
8.			
9.			
10.			
11.			
12.			
13.			
14.			
15.			
16.			
17.			
18.			
19.			
20.			

Practice Electronic Search

Directions: Use your electronic catalog to practice doing a search for a title, author, or subject. Write the choices that appear on the screen for each search.

1. Title

_____

_____

_____

_____

2. Subject

_____

_____

_____

_____

3. Author

_____

_____

_____

4. Key Word

_____

_____

_____

_____

NAME _____   DATE _____

Research Skills

Your teacher has assigned a research project that will need a visit to the library media center.

1. Where will you begin your search in the library media center?

2. What are the four ways you can search for information using the card catalog or electronic database?

   a.

   b.

   c.

   d.

3. How are authors' names listed in the card catalog or electronic card catalog?

4. How do you find subject information in the card catalog or electronic database?

5. The Dewey classification numbers are used for what kind of books?

6. Why do you use a call slip?

7. Write the information you would need to find a book that you have written. You should be able to locate it four ways.

NAME _____ DATE _____

Which Is Best?

Directions: Here are the results of doing an electronic search for the subject of "snakes." Read each entry and answer the questions that follow.

Barger, Sherie, 1944- *Copperheads*/Sherie Bargar, Linda Johnson;
Photographer/consultant George Van Horn. Vero Beach, Fla.: Rourke, © 1986.
JUV BOOK 597.96BAR (Vol. 1)
JUV BOOK 597.96BAR (Vol. 2)
An introduction to the physical characteristics, habitats, natural environment, and relationship to human beings of the various species of copperheads.

Cannon, Janell, 1957 *Verdi* [author & illustrator] Janell Cannon 1st ed. San Diego, Calif.:
Harcourt Brace © 1997
PICTUREBK E CAN
A young python does not want to grow slow and boring like the older snakes he sees in the tropical jungle where he lives.

Hall, Katy. *Snakey riddles*/by Katy Hall and Lisa Eisenberg; pictures by Simms Taback. 1st ed. New York: Dial Books for Young Readers, © 1990.
JUVBOOK 793.7HAL
An illustrated collection of riddles about snakes, including "What kind of snake can you find on the front of your car? A windshield viper!"

1. If you were doing a report on snakes, which book would you find most helpful?

2. Explain your answer for question 1.

3. Jim's mom is looking for a picture book for her six-year-old. Which book do you think she should borrow from the library?

4. How did you decide on the answer to question 3?

5. How do you know where to find the snake riddle book?

NAME _____   DATE _____

Match Author, Subject, and Title

You have a mixed-up set of cards from the card catalog. Match the author's name with the subject and title of his or her book. Write the number with the author's name in the blanks before the related subject and title.

Author	**Subject**	**Title**
1. Rey, H. A.	_9_ numbers	___ *The Sorcerer's Stone*
2. Brown, Marc	___ school	___ *Tom Sawyer* and *Huckleberry Finn*
3. Allard, Harry	___ fairy tales	___ *Curious George Visits the Zoo*
4. Emberley, Ed	___ holidays	___ *The New Kid on the Block*
5. Twain, Mark	___ monkeys	___ *The Great Thumbprint Drawing*
6. Prelutsky, Jack	___ wizards	___ *Abraham Lincoln*
7. Briggs, Raymond	___ river adventure	___ *Miss Nelson Is Missing*
8. Rowling, J. K.	___ poetry	_9_ *Anno's Counting Book*
9. Anno, Mitsumasa	___ art	___ *Snow White*
10. Grimm, Wilhelm	___ winter	___ *The Snowman*
11. D'Aulaire, Ingri	___ biography	___ *Arthur's Thanksgiving*

Pass the Torch (Tic-Tac-Toe)

Directions: Students use knowledge of library layout and tic-tac-toe to play this game.

1. Divide the students into teams.

2. Give each team at least three cards to begin the game. Students may also have printouts from the electronic card catalog.

    a. Card one lists a book title.

    b. Card two lists an author's name.

    c. Card three lists a subject. Subject cards may have several suitable titles, which can all be used.

    d. Additional cards list author, title, or subject.

3. The teams compete against each other to locate books using the three cards, and/or electronic card catalog information to locate the books.

4. Students retrieve the books and place them in the tic-tac-toe grid.

The tic-tac-toe grid is made by placing strips of colored paper on a table. Teams place a book in the grid to claim the square.

The first team to have books in three squares in a row becomes the winner.

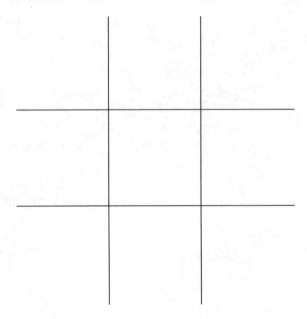

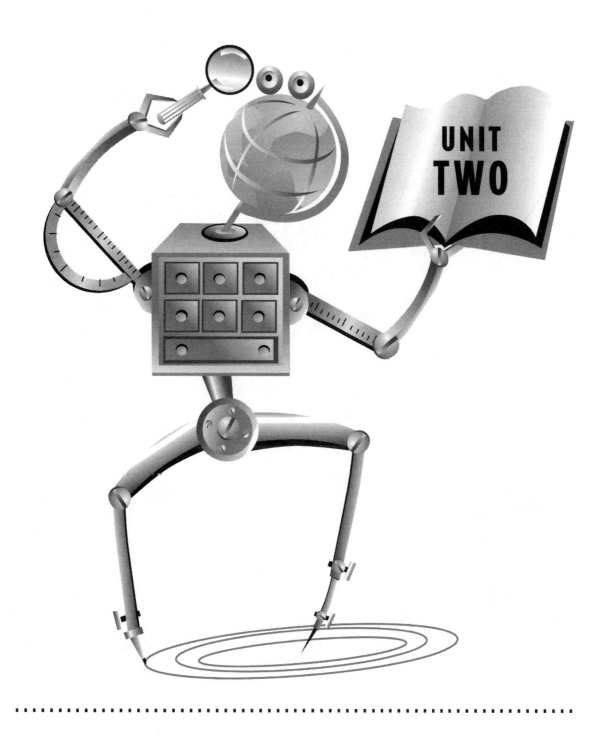

UNIT
TWO

Using Reference Resources

LESSON 2-A

Learning and Using the Parts of a Reference Book

To the Instructor ....

Do your students have difficulty using books efficiently? In this lesson, students will become familiar with the parts of a book, will learn how to use those parts to locate topics, and will learn how to determine the meaning of words used in a book.

Objectives ....

Students will learn

1. How to identify the purpose of each part of a reference book.

2. How to use a table of contents.

3. Why a book is divided into chapters.

4. How to use the index to locate subjects and topics included in the book.

5. How to apply the glossary for meanings of words used in the book.

Materials ....

Transparencies

2.1 Sample Book Pages ☐ ◧ ■

2.2 Parts of a Book ☐ ◧ ■

Books containing tables of contents, multiple chapters, indexes, and glossaries

Teaching and Preparation ....

1. Display the major parts of a book.

   Title page: page at the front of the book that tells the name of the book and other information including the author and publisher

   Copyright page: page that tells when the book was published; often on the back of the title page

   Table of contents: a listing of everything contained in the book, which normally includes divisions called chapters, often with subtopics

   Body: the main part of the book

   Glossary: an alphabetical list of terms and difficult words used in the book, with definitions

   Index: an alphabetical list of names and subjects together with page numbers on which they appear in the text

   Appendix: added information about topics in the body of the book

   Chapters: divisions of a book allowing the author to address a new subject or episode

2. Demonstrate how to use a table of contents to find a chapter, index, or glossary.

3. Explain how to use the glossary.

4. Describe how to use the index to locate subjects and the pages on which they appear.

5. Review Internet references.

   http://www.yahooligans.com/reference/factbook

   http://www.yahooligans.com/reference/weights_and_measures

   http://www.bartleby.com/

   http://www.bartleby.com/reference

   http://www.xrefer.com

Activity ....

Use LMC materials to locate parts of books (no page) □ ◧ ■

Worksheets ....

2.1 Book Parts I □ ◧ ■

2.2 Book Parts II ◧ ■

Games . . . .

2.1 The Parts Game ▯▮ ■

2.2 Stump the Student ☐ ▯▮ ■

Connections to the Curriculum . . . .

All areas of the curriculum use the table of contents, indexes, glossaries, and so on. Use an encyclopedia index to locate specific information.

Art—artists (Monet, Cézanne, Picasso, Warhol)

Language arts—reading chapter books

Math—architecture

Music—genres of music (opera, rap, country, classical)

Physical education—sports (football, baseball, tennis)

Science—inventions (telephone, computer, automobile)

Social studies—national symbols (Statue of Liberty, Washington Monument)

Answer Key . . . .

WORKSHEET 2.1

Table of Contents	Body	Index	Glossary
1 5 9	3 8	2 6	4 7

WORKSHEET 2.2

1. contents
2. copyright
3. title
4. copyright
5. index
6. title
7. contents
8. index
9. title
10. contents
11. title
12. contents
13. index
14. glossary
15. contents
16. index
17. title
18. glossary
19. index
20. contents

Sample Book Pages

Title Page

Name of the book

Language Learning

by John Doe

Prentice Hall, New Jersey

Table of Contents

Listing of all that is contained in the book

Glossary

Alphabetical list of terms, with definitions, that are used in the book

Adjective   A word used to modify a noun

Noun   A word used to denote a person, place, or thing

Index

Alphabetical list of names and subjects with the page numbers on which they appear in the text

Adjectives, 27

Adverbs, 16

Capital letters, 25

Nouns, 33

Pronouns, 33

Punctuation, 26

Sentence, 25

Body

These pages tell the story or teach the lesson.

TRANSPARENCY 2.1

Parts of a Book

The main part of the book is called the **body** of the book.

An **appendix** is at the back of a book. It contains information that the author would like you to refer to in the book. It might contain charts, tables, lists of resources, and so on

A **glossary** is like a mini-dictionary and follows the appendix. It allows you to check words or terms you are uncertain of without reading an entire chapter to find them.

The **index** is the final part of the book. It is an alphabetical listing of all the important or key subjects discussed in the book. You will also find names or titles discussed in the book.

The **copyright page** is usually on the back side of the **title page**. The page tells you when the book was copyrighted, and who published it.

To use magazines effectively use the *Children's Magazine Guide* (published by R. R. Bowker).

The guide is arranged by subject alphabetically. The headings are in all capital letters in bold-faced type. First look for the topic. The cross reference will tell you where to find more information. The note will give you additional information about the article. Sometimes the magazines are abbreviated. The full name can be found on the inside cover. After the page number you may see a "+." This means that the article is continued later in the magazine.

Use a **Newspaper Index.**

Every newspaper has an index, which is a list of articles and columns in alphabetical order. An **article** is a newspaper story. A **column** is a short article written regularly by the same person. Articles and columns are in **sections**. Each section is given a letter. The page numbers will follow the section letters.

 TRANSPARENCY 2.2

Book Parts I

Table of Contents	Body	Index	Glossary

Directions: Do you know where to find the following entries? Place the information in the column above that is the best category.

1. Punctuating sentences   56

2. Nouns, 20

3. Once upon a time …

4. **Fiction**   Made up, imaginary

5. LEARNING MATH

6. Bicycles, 66

7. **Theme**   The central idea in literature

8. Someday my prince will come

9. Newspapers   58

NAME _____   DATE _____

Book Parts II

Directions: Write "title," "copyright," "contents," "glossary," or "index" on the line opposite the entries you would find in a book.

1. Unit 2 The Thirteen Colonies 221   _____

2. Printed in New York, New York   _____

3. by Gina Christine   _____

4. copyright © 2002   _____

5. Clydesdale. *See* horses   _____

6. *Penguins* by Ryan Patrick   _____

7. Index 27   _____

8. snail mail, 13   _____

9. *Looking for the Perfect Picture*   _____

10. Chapter 5 Caring for Cats and Kittens   _____

11. Lucky Publishing Co., Fortune, Utah   _____

12. Part 4: Myths and Legends   _____

13. Telephone; *see also* communication   _____

14. calf: a baby cow   _____

15. Lesson 7 Learning How to Cha Cha   _____

16. charts and maps, 16–19, 302–309   _____

17. Edited by Edward Joseph   _____

18. Midnight—Twelve o'clock A.M.   _____

19. Photography, 31   _____

20. What Now? How to say it in Spanish 12   _____

The Parts Game

Materials

One die for a group of three or four players
Library books or subject texts; one for each player
Bookmark sets, cut apart
Pencils or pens

Rules

Team member rolls the die. Place the bookmark in a book according to how the die falls; 1 = Body, 2 = Chapter, and so on (lower grades). Students in higher grades will place the bookmark and record answers to the questions on it. Points are earned by placing the bookmark correctly and recording the correct answers. Answers are checked by peers.

Bookmarks

Body (1)	Chapters (2)	Glossary (3)	Index (4)	Table of Contents (5)	Title (6)
Last page minus First page divided by 2 equals Middle page #	Chapter with *most* pages Chapter with *least* pages	First word Last word	Locate entry with* _____ *See also Diagram* [word] *Write the subject topic for the reference.	First chapter/unit begins on page ___ Last chapter/unit begins on page ___ Number of chapters/units ___	Write title _____ Write author _____ What is the copyright date? _____

Stump the Student

Materials

Stacks of books *used* by the students to make their "Stump the Student" cards.

Stacks of books to *confuse* the other team.

Rules

1. Students prepare their "Stump the Student" cards by writing *clues* of partial titles and author names; copyright year or publishing company; entries from a glossary, table of contents, or index on the appropriate lines plus the books they are from on the *left* part. They write only the clues on the *right* part.

2. Students will select a "Stump the Student" challenge sheet and work as a team or individually.

3. Students will locate the correct book from the clues. The students or teams who finish first with the most correct locations are the winners.

Left: stumper with *correct answer*   Right: stumper only for students to locate

Stump the Student	**Stump the Student**
Locate a book with . . .	Locate a book with . . .
Title	**Title**
Book _____	Book _____
Author	**Author**
Book _____	Book _____
Copyright	**Copyright**
Book _____	Book _____
Table of Contents	**Table of Contents**
Book _____	Book _____
Index	**Index**
Book _____	Book _____
Glossary	**Glossary**
Book _____	Book _____

LESSON 2-B

. . . .

How to Use a Table of Contents

To the Instructor . . . .

How can students find out if a book is right for them at a glance? They can look at the table of contents.

Objectives . . . .

1. Students learn how to use the table of contents of books to select relevant material for research purposes.

2. Students learn how to locate information on specific pages using the table of contents of a book.

Materials . . . .

Transparency

2.3 Table of Contents ☐ ◧ ■

Books with a table of contents

Teaching and Preparation

1. Display table of contents from different books.

2. Demonstrate how to use a table of contents to find a chapter, the index, or the glossary.

3. Demonstrate how to use a table of contents to locate the first and last pages of chapters, of the index, and of the glossary.

4. Review Internet reference

   http://www.factmonster.com/homework/t5organize.html

Activities

2.1 Using the Table of Contents and Index I □ ◧ ■

2.2 Using the Table of Contents and Index II □ ◧ ■

Worksheets

2.3 Table of Contents and Index I ◧ ■

2.4 Table of Contents and Index II ◧ ■

2.5 Table of Contents and Index III □ ◧

2.6 Chapters □ ◧

Connections to the Curriculum

All reference books have a table of contents page.

Answer Key

ACTIVITIES 2.1 AND 2.2

Answers will vary.

WORKSHEET 2.3

1. Language Arts
2. 25
3. 24
4. Chapter 3
5. Chapter 3
6. 45
7. No, basics only
8. Front of books
9. Back of books
10. Index

WORKSHEET 2.4

1. Location, amount of information
2. Back of books
3. Front of books
4. Index
5. Table of contents
6. Index
7. Index
8. Easy location of information
9. Order of presentation
10. 26
11. Index

WORKSHEET 2.5

1. Back of books
2. Front of books
3. Specific
4. General
5. Index
6. Table of contents
7. Index
8. Index
9. Easy location of information
10. Order of presentation

WORKSHEET 2.6

1. Born on the Fourth of July
2. Where Is My Rattle?
3. I'm Two Today
4. Kindergarten Is Fun
5. My Second Grade Class
6. First Day of High School
7. Old Enough to Drive?
8. Graduation from College
9. No More School, Get a Job
10. Retire to Florida

Table of Contents

A

Table of Contents

Contents Overview

B

Contents

 **TRANSPARENCY 2.3**

Transparency Questions

The accompanying transparency showed the table of contents for a fiction (A) and a nonfiction (B) book. Similarities are shown. Each page shows where divisions of books begin and end.

1. **Which contents page is for a nonfiction book, A or B?**

   B

2. **Which contents page is for a fiction book, A or B?**

   A

3. **How are the contents pages alike?**

   There are divisions of a book shown with the pages on which the divisions begin.

4. **How are they different?**

   The divisions of the book are called chapters or sections.

5. **How many pages are in Chapter One?**

   The chapter begins on page 8 and the next chapter begins on page 13. To find out how many pages are in the chapter subtract 8 from 13, to get 5 pages.

6. **How many pages are in Section 1?**

   Section 1 begins on page 2 and the next section begins on page 30. To find out how many pages are in the section subtract 2 from 30, to get 28 pages.

7. **Are all of the units numbered the same way?**

   Roman numerals are used in the numbering along with Arabic numerals.

Using the Table of Contents and Index I

Directions: Use books with similar formats, such as tables of contents and indexes. Animal book sets, state book sets, and country book sets are excellent for this activity.

Students may complete this activity either individually or in teams. If this is an individual activity, each student will need a book from the book set. If there are limited numbers of books, divide the class into teams of two or three students and distribute animal, state, or country books to each team.

Students shall use the index and table of contents of their books to locate answers to these questions. They need to write the answer and page number on their paper. Answers will vary according to the resource used.

The individual or team with the most correct answers in the shortest time will be the winner.

Animal Books

Name of animal to be researched _____

1. What food does your animal eat? _____ Page _____

2. Where does your animal live? _____ Page _____

3. What are you animal's enemies? _____ Page _____

4. What does your animal look like (picture)? _____ Page _____

5. What are two (2) interesting facts about your animal?

   a. _____ Page _____

   b. _____ Page _____

Using the Table of Contents and Index II

Directions: Use books with similar formats, such as tables of contents and indexes. Animal book sets, state book sets, and country book sets are excellent for this activity.

Students may complete this activity either individually or in teams. If this is an individual activity, each student will need a book from the book set. If there are limited numbers of books, divide the class into teams of two or three students and distribute animal, state, or country books to each team.

Students shall use the index and table of contents of their books to locate answers to these questions. They need to write the answer and page number on their paper. Answers will vary according to the resource used.

The individual or team with the most correct answers in the shortest time will be the winner.

State/Country Books

Name of state or country to be researched _____

1. What is the capital? _____ Page _____

2. How large is your state/country (land area)? _____ Page _____

3. What is the population of your state/country? _____ Page _____

4. What natural resources (coal, oil, uranium, etc.) are most abundant

   in your state/country? _____ Page _____

5. What are two (2) interesting facts about your state/country?

   a. _____ Page _____

   b. _____ Page _____

NAME _____   DATE _____

Table of Contents and Index I

Directions: Look at the table of contents and index below, then answer the questions.

Contents		Index
	Page	
Chapter 1		adjectives, 27
Learn the Alphabet	4	adverbs, 16
Chapter 2		capital letters, 25
Three-Letter Words	7	nouns, 33
Chapter 3		pronouns, 33
Write Sentences	25	punctuation, 26
Chapter 4		sentence, 2
Paragraphs	39	
Index	45	

1. What kind of book will have the contents and index pages as shown above?

2. On what page does Chapter 3 begin?

3. On what page does Chapter 2 end?

4. In which chapter would you find "pronouns"?

5. In which chapter would you find "adjectives"?

6. On what page does the index begin?

7. Can you learn how to write a fairy tale using this book?

8. Where is the table of contents located in a book?

9. Where is the index located in a book?

10. Would it be better to use the table of contents or index to find a particular subject?

Table of Contents and Index II

Directions: Answer the questions about the table of contents and index of a book.

1. Compare the index and the table of contents of a book.

2. Where is the index located?

3. Where is the table of contents located?

4. Where will you find more detailed information—the table of contents or the index?

5. Where will you find more specific facts?

6. You have a specific topic to search for. Which will help you get the information more quickly and easily?

7. You need to skim the book for a specific detail for your reports. Where do you go?

8. Why is the index written in alphabetical order?

9. How is the table of contents organized?

10. On what page might you read about question marks and commas?

11. Would you use the table of contents or index to find this information?

Contents		**Index**
	Page	
Chapter 1		adjectives, 27
Learn the Alphabet	4	adverbs, 16
Chapter 2		capital letters, 25
Three-Letter Words	7	nouns, 33
Chapter 3		pronouns, 33
Write Sentences	25	punctuation, 26
Chapter 4		sentence, 2
Paragraphs	39	
Index	45	

Table of Contents and Index III

Directions: Answer the following questions about tables of contents and indexes.

1. Where is the index located?

2. Where is the table of contents located?

3. Name the kind of information found in an index.

4. What kind of information is available in the table of contents?

5. Where will you find more detailed information—the table of contents or the index?

6. Where will you find big ideas and breakdowns of the main ideas?

7. You have a specific topic to search for. Which will help you get the information more quickly and easily, the table of contents or the index?

8. Are the page numbers listed in the table of contents or in the index more helpful to find specific information?

9. Why is the index written in alphabetical order?

10. How is the table of contents organized?

Chapters

Directions: A computer problem mixed up this table of contents. Can you unscramble the titles of this autobiography book called *This Is My Life*? Write the titles in the correct chronological order on the lines for each chapter.

Graduation from College   **I'm Two Today**   **First Day of High School**

Kindergarten Is Fun   **Where Is My Rattle?**   **No More School, Get a Job**

My Second Grade Class   **Old Enough to Drive?**

Retire to Florida   **Born on the Fourth of July**

Table of Contents

This Is My Life

Chapter 1
_____

Chapter 2
_____

Chapter 3
_____

Chapter 4
_____

Chapter 5
_____

Chapter 6
_____

Chapter 7
_____

Chapter 8
_____

Chapter 9
_____

Chapter 10
_____

LESSON 2-C

How to Use an Index

To the Instructor

This section is to help students learn how to use print and electronic indexes. The first and best place to learn about indexes is a reference book. Some search engines use the index principle.

Objectives

1. Students observe how all indexes are alike.

2. Students notice that all reference indexes are in alphabetical order.

3. Students learn how to locate information using an index.

4. Students learn how to use an Internet index search engine.

Materials

Transparency

2.4 Using Indexes ☐ ◨ ■

Books with indexes
Internet computers with Yahoo or a similar index search engine

Teaching and Preparation ....

1. Demonstrate the different parts of an index.

2. Locate a topic in the index and turn to pages in the text.

3. Use a search engine index such as Yahoo and demonstrate similarities.

4. Review Internet references.

   http://www.yahoo.com

   http://www.yahooligans.com

   http://www.lii.org

Activities ....

2.3 Using Indexes ▯■ ■

Search animal and state books by table of contents (no page) ☐ ▯■ ■

Worksheet ....

2.7 Index ☐ ▯■ ■

Connections to the Curriculum ....

Use textbook indexes daily to locate information.

Answer Key ....

ACTIVITY 2.3

Answers will vary.

WORKSHEET 2.7

1. 7 pages
2. 33 pages
3. Jefferson City;
   Kansas City; St. Louis;
   Truman, Harry S

4. Alphabetically
5. Looking in another
   section of the book
   for more information

6. States
7. Two

Using Indexes

Print Index

Boldface—Index heading

Word(s)—Index entry, lightface

[Word]—brackets—Identifier (description)

(Words)—parentheses—Article subheading

B:136—Volume (encyclopedia or multivolume set and page number)

With diagram—italics—Illustration indication

See also—italics—Cross-reference

Encyclopedia

Index entries in all capital **boldface** indicate subjects on which the encyclopedia has an individual article.

Boldface capital and small letters are used for three kinds of entries.

1. The initial word or phrase of a cross-reference that directs the reader to one or more articles in the encyclopedia.
2. Members of a family with the same name who are grouped together in one article.
3. Entries without volume, page, or column reference.

   Entries in lightface type indicate subjects on which the encyclopedia has no separate articles. The volume, page, and column references indicate discussion within other articles.

   Index entries in italic type indicate species and genera of plants and animals, foreign terms, musical compositions, literary works, periodicals, works of art, and ships.

   Indented entries in lightface capital letters appearing under an article title indicate other articles of the encyclopedia in which significant additional information on the subject can be found.

   Indented entries in lightface small letters appearing under an article title indicate subsections within that article and related information from other articles.

   Index entries are arranged in alphabetical order.

   Cross-reference entries indicate alternate spellings or titles or those subjects that are not discussed in individual articles.

   The a and b in an entry denote which column an entry is located in.

Electronic Index

1. Electronic indexes work on the entry, which is the word you wish to search.
2. Type the entry word in the search box and press enter. The "hits" appear as a list, which is the index to locating the specific information.
3. Entries are in colors that when clicked take you to the site for the article.
4. Boldface words in the index add links working from the general to the specific.
5. Instead of turning pages, a click of the mouse locates the information listed in the index.

Yahoo and Yahooligans are examples of a search engine index (http://www.yahooligans.com).

 **TRANSPARENCY 2.4**

Using Indexes

Print Index

Boldface—Index heading

Word(s)—Index entry, lightface

[Word]—brackets—Identifier (description)

(Words)—parentheses—Article subheading

B:136—Volume (encyclopedia or multivolume set and page number)

With diagram—italics—Illustration indication

See also—italics—Cross-reference

Electronic Index

Yahoo and Yahooligans are examples of a search engine index.
http://www.yahooligans.com

Directions: Students use print and electronic indexes to find answers to the following questions.

1. Encyclopedia index: Locate information about the state you live in. Write the volume and page number.

2. Subject book: [birds] Find information about your state bird. Learn what the state bird is from reading the article in the encyclopedia about your state.

3. Curriculum text: [social studies] Find a map of your state. Write the page number and the kind of map it is.

4. Yahooligans: Access information about the governor of your state. Write his or her name and where he or she lives.

Index

An index is a search tool. Some search engines on the Internet are also indexes. Specific terms, people, and places are listed alphabetically with the page numbers where the terms may be found in the textbook.

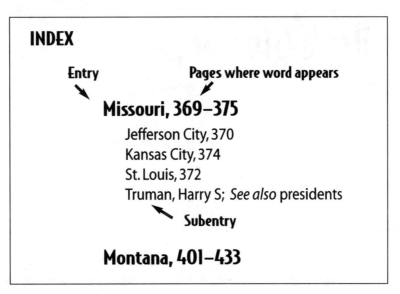

INDEX

Entry   Pages where word appears

Missouri, 369–375

Jefferson City, 370
Kansas City, 374
St. Louis, 372
Truman, Harry S; *See also* presidents

Subentry

Montana, 401–433

Directions: Refer to the sample index card above and answer the following questions.

1. How many pages are on the topic of Missouri?

2. How many pages are on the topic of Montana?

3. List the subentries.

4. How are the subentries organized?

5. What does the entry with "*See also* presidents" suggest?

6. What do you think this reference book might be about?

7. How many entries are seen in the sample?

LESSON 2-D

How to Use a Glossary

To the Instructor ....

Do your students get confused with words and their definitions found in reference books? A specialized dictionary at the end of a reference book defines terms.

Objectives ....

1. Students recognize that the definitions of terms used in a reference book can be found in the glossary of reference books.

2. Students learn how to locate definitions of unfamiliar terms used in the text.

Materials ....

Transparency

2.5 Glossary ☐ ◧ ■

Books with glossaries

Teaching and Preparation ....

1. Compare glossaries, dictionaries, thesauri, and other reference books using guide words to locate words.

2. Read the text and stop to look up unfamiliar words in the glossary.

3. Review Internet references.

http://www.google.com/search?hl=en&q=glossary

http://www.glossarist.com (Glossarist)

http://www.poeticbyway.com/glossary.html (Glossary of poetic terms)

Worksheets . . . .

2.8 Guide Words in the Glossary ☐ ◧

2.9 Glossary and Guide Words ☐ ◧

2.10 Do You Know? ☐ ◧ ■

2.11 My Own Glossary ☐ ◧ ■

Connections to the Curriculum . . . .

Students need to know the vocabulary of each subject.

Answer Key . . . .

TRANSPARENCY 2.5

Door, dots, dopey, doo-wop
Scout, second, scraps, shark

WORKSHEET 2.8

Renew, remove, repair, relief
Heel, hefty, hedge, hectoliter
Chicago, chemistry, cherry, chicken
Skin, skeleton, soap, slug, smooth, snicker

WORKSHEET 2.9

1. The glossary is in the back of the book.
2. Words in the glossary are special and unusual words in that book.
3. Guide words limit the search to words alphabetically listed in between them.

cat = cast-catch	jam = jacket-Japan	here = herb-heritage
canary = 0	heaven = head-help	captain = canvas-captive
jokes = join-journal		

WORKSHEET 2.10

1. A glossary is in the back of a book.
2. The key word is in boldface.
3. The glossary gives definitions.
4. The glossary contains key words, definitions, and page numbers.*
5. The author lists the words.
6. Yes, it is found in the dictionary and index volumes in a set.
7. Yes
8. Yes, for ease of locating terms
9. It would be easy to locate if the page number were included, but not otherwise.

   *Some glossaries include page location, others do not.

WORKSHEET 2.11

Answers will vary.

Glossary

The glossary is located at the end of books. It is an alphabetical listing of words with definitions that are used in a particular book. Glossaries and dictionaries operate under the same rules. Guide words are used in some large glossaries.

Glossary		**and**	**Dictionary**	
Guide Word	Guide Word		Guide Word	Guide Word

Key term in **bold** *Definition or Description*

↙

Definitions on page begin with the left guide word and end with the right guide word. (p. 301)

Same as Glossary

Page where term is used (not in all glossaries)

The first two words in the following boxes are the guide words. Which words in the lists beneath them will you find on the same glossary page?

---

doodle/double

door   does   dots   dog   dopey   donut   doctor   doo-wop   domino

---

school/sheep

scout   scamp   second   sheet   science   scraps   shark

NAME _____ DATE _____

Guide Words in the Glossary

Are you able to locate words in a glossary quickly? Entries in dictionaries and glossaries are in alphabetical order. *Guide words* are used to maximize searching. Guide words are words printed at the top of a page in a dictionary, glossary, and encyclopedia. The left guide word is the first entry on the page. The right guide word shows the last entry on the page.

Procedure

Turn the pages of your dictionary, glossary, and/or encyclopedia, looking at the guide words at the top of each page.

Practice

Directions: In each of the following boxes, circle the words in the second line that would appear on the page with the guide words above them.

---

relative/repeat

renew   reject   remove   repair   regain   reindeer   register   relief

---

heavy/height

heel   heaven   heat   hefty   hedge   head   health   hectoliter   hem

---

chef/chili

chop   Chicago   chemistry   cherry   checker   chicken   chapter   chip

---

skate/soda

skin   size   skeleton   soap   slug   silver   smooth   snicker   soft

---

NAME _____   DATE _____

Glossary and Guide Words

Directions: Answer the questions about the glossary.

1. Where is the glossary in a book?

2. What words will you find in the glossary?

3. Why do you need guide words?

Directions: Draw a line to connect each word in column A with its guide words. One word in column A and one set in column B do not have a match.

A	Guide Words
cat	herb-heritage
canary	head-help
jokes	catfish-caught
jam	cast-catch
heaven	join-journal
here	jacket-Japan
captain	canvas-captive

WORKSHEET 2.10

NAME   DATE

Do You Know?

Do you know the meaning of all the words used in the book you are reading? A glossary is a specialized mini-dictionary found at the back of a subject book. It explains key words, new words, or difficult words found in the body of the book. The alphabetical order allows you to find information quickly. Sometimes the specialized vocabulary is listed at the beginning of a chapter.

Directions: Answer the questions about glossaries.

1. Where is a glossary located?

2. How can you tell the key word (entry) from the definition?

3. How is a glossary different from an index?

4. What information about a word will be found in the glossary?

5. Who chooses the words printed in the glossary?

6. Is a glossary found in the back of an encyclopedia?

7. Is a glossary found in a math book?

8. Are the terms in the glossary in alphabetical order? Why?

9. Would it be easy or difficult to locate the page on which a glossary word is used in the text pages? Why, or why not?

76

My Own Glossary

Directions: Select an article from a magazine or newspaper. Skim the story. Make a list of vocabulary words that you feel should be listed in a glossary for that story. Write a definition for each word and draw a picture to illustrate what the word means.

Name of article or story _____

Source for story or article _____

Words and definitions in alphabetical order _____

_____

_____

_____

_____

_____

Variation

Directions: Find an unfamiliar word in a newspaper or magazine. Use the boxes below to record the word and guess what you think it means from the context, then look up the word in a dictionary and record the actual definition. Compare the two in the final box on the right.

Unfamiliar Word	Guess Meaning from Context	Actual Definition	Difference

LESSON 2-E

How to Use a Bibliography

To the Instructor ....

How does a student give credit when he or she has used a book or some other reference material? A bibliography gives credit where credit is due.

Objectives ....

1. Students learn the purpose of a bibliography.
2. Students write complete bibliographies.

Materials ....

Transparency

2.6 Correct Ways to Cite Resources ☐ ◧ ◼

Copies of bibliography pages
Sample materials to practice writing bibliographies

Teaching and Preparation ....

1. Demonstrate how to locate information for a bibliography.

2. Practice writing bibliography information.

3. Review Internet references.

   http://www.yahooligans.com/content/ask_earl

   http://www.liu.edu/cwis/cwp/library/workshop/citation.htm

   www.askyahoo.com/ask/20020510.html

Activities ....

Cut apart bibliography information to practice arranging on a pocket chart or magnetic board. (no page) ☐ ◧ ■

Keep one part out of a citing and have students decide what information is missing to complete the citing. (no page) ☐ ◧ ■

Worksheets ....

2.12 Writing Bibliographies ◧ ■

2.13 Understanding Bibliographies ☐ ◧

Connections to the Curriculum ....

Anytime a student needs to write a report he or she should include a bibliography to confirm the resources used to do the work.

Answer Key ....

WORKSHEET 2.12

Bridge, Gina. *Poetry of the People.* London, England: Rugget & Co., 1967.

Kloster, Edward. *History of Ireland.* Kansas City: Perry Publishing, 1939.

Moore, Margaret, Ph.D. "Sisters Forever." *The Irish Encyclopedia.* New York: Calvary, Inc., 2002.

Songs of the Emerald Isle. Videocassette. By Bridget Britain. (Dir. Joseph Barbados). North & Sons, 1996.

Swears, Virginia. *Children's Games.* Boston: Polish Publishing, 2000.

Tierney, Ryan. *The Luck of the Irish.* Osage Beach: Penguin Books, 1994.

The topic covered by these resources is Ireland and its history of children's entertainment, including songs, games, and poetry.

WORKSHEET 2.13

1. A bibliography is a list of the materials used to research a topic.
2. The author's name is listed alphabetically by last name.
3. The title of the work is always underlined or italicized.
4. Quotation marks are used for titles of newspaper, magazine, and encyclopedia articles. Filmstrips and television programs may also be enclosed in quotation marks.
5. The punctuation at the end of bibliographic citations is a period.
6. Punctuation is necessary in writing every bibliographic citation.
7. Pamphlets
8. Newspapers
9. Copyright is an official notification that the author's ideas are solely his or her possession and must be given credit.
10. Answers will vary.

Correct Ways to Cite Resources

The bibliography is included at the end of your paper and is arranged alphabetically by the first word in the citation, usually the author's name. If the author's name is unknown, alphabetize by the first word in the title other than "a," "an," or "the." Note that the punctuation is important and part of the citing.

Print

Books

> Author's last name, author's first name or initial. *Title of the Book.* City: Publisher, copyright date.

Pamphlet

> Same as book

Magazine article

> Author's last name, author's first name or initial. "Title of the Article." *Name of the Magazine,* volume (date of the magazine), page numbers.

Newspaper

> Same as magazine

Encyclopedia (printed or CD-ROM)

> (Look at the end of the article to find the author's name.)

> Author's last name, author's first name or initial. "Title of Article." *Name of Encyclopedia.* Publisher, year of edition.

Letter

> Name of person writing letter. Letter. Person receiving letter. Date.

Nonprint

Personal interview

> (Name of person talked to) Last name, first name. Personal interview. Telephone interview. Date of interview.

TRANSPARENCY 2.6

Electronic Citations

Website citation

Author's last name, author's first name or initial (if any). *Title of Site.* [Online] Available http://internet address, date you last visited the site.

E-mail message

Author of e-mail message. *Subject of the Message* [Online] Available e-mail: name@domain name, date of message.

Encyclopedia article from CD-ROM

"Title of Article." *Title of CD-ROM.* CD-ROM. Publisher. Year.

Encyclopedia article on the Web

Author's last name, author's first name or initial. "Title of Article." *Encyclopedia Title.* Date of visit to site <URL of article>.

Magazine article from CD-ROM

Author's last name, author's first name or initial. "Title of Article." *Periodical Title.* Month and date of article, year: *Database Title.* CD-ROM. Name of service provider, date.

Magazine article on the Web

Author's last name, author's first name or initial. "Title of Article." *Original source of article.* Date of original source: page numbers. Product name. Date of visit to site <URL of article>.

Software

Title of Software. Computer software publisher, copyright date. Type of computer format.

Telnet

Author. Title of telnet item. Date of document or download telnet://address.path.

Videocassette program

Title of Program. Videocassette. By [author's name]. (Dir. [director's name]). Network, copyright date.

Filmstrip

"Title of Filmstrip," *Title of the Complete Works—Series.* (Filmstrip). Place of publication. Producer, copyright date.

Television Program

"Title of the Episode." Prod. [producer's name]. Dir. [Director's name]. Network, date of air.

 **TRANSPARENCY 2.6 cont.**

NAME _____   DATE _____

Writing Bibliographies

The word *bibliography* comes from the Latin word *biblio*. *Biblio* means "book," and the word *graph* means "write." A bibliography is a written list of books and resources used for a report on a particular topic. All the materials are listed alphabetically according to the author's last name or the title, and the bibliography usually includes at least five facts about each book: the author, the title, the place of publication, the publishing company, and the date of publication.

Directions: Using these author cards, write a bibliography.

Author Cards

Tierney, Ryan The Luck of the Irish Osage Beach Penguin Books, 1994	Britain, Bridget Songs of the Emerald Isle Videocassette Barbados, Joseph, Director North & Sons, 1996	Kloster, Edward History of Ireland Kansas City Perry Publishing, 1939
Bridge, Gina Poetry of the People London, England Rugget & Co., 1967	Swears, Virginia Children's Games Boston Polish Publishing, 2000	Moore, Margaret, Ph.D. Sisters Forever The Irish Encyclopedia New York Calvary, Inc., 2002

Bibliography

What is the topic of this report? _____

NAME _____   DATE _____

Understanding Bibliographies

1. What is a bibliography?

2. How do you write the author's name in a bibliography?

3. What is always underlined or italicized?

4. When do you use quotation marks?

5. What do all bibliographic citations end with?

6. Is punctuation important in writing a bibliography?

7. Books and _____ use the same form for citations.

8. Magazines and _____ use the same form for citations.

9. What is a copyright?

10. Write the bibliography for a book you are pretending you are going to write.

Using Reference Resources: General Information

LESSON 3-A

··

Almanac

To the Instructor ···

Where can students find recent statistics and information? Almanacs are published yearly. They provide brief, accurate information on an endless assortment of subjects.

Objectives ···

1. Students learn the history of the almanac.

2. Students learn how to access information available in a print almanac.

3. Students learn how to access an online almanac for information.

Materials ···

Transparency

3.1 Almanac ▯▮ ▮

Classroom set of almanacs

Teaching and Preparation ....

1. Demonstrate how to use a print almanac.

2. Access the *Old Farmer's Almanac* Website. http://www.almanac.com/history/history.html

3. Review Internet references.

   http://www.almanac.com

   http://www.infoplease.com (Information Please)

   http://www.farmersalmanac.com (Old Farmer's Almanac)

   http://www.freepint.com/gary/handbook.htm (Fast Facts)

   http://www.50states.com (50 states and links)

Activities ....

3.1 Almanac Scavenger Hunt ◨ ■

3.2 Almanac Research ◨ ■

Worksheets ....

3.1 Planet Search ☐ ◨ ■

3.2 States Search ☐ ◨ ■

3.3 *Old Farmers Almanac* ☐ ◨ ■

Game ....

3.1 Please ... The Answer ◨ ■

Connections to the Curriculum ....

Physical Education—sports records
Science—weather information
Social studies—the day in history, special days, current events

Answer Key ....

ACTIVITIES 3.1 AND 3.2

Answers will vary.

WORKSHEET 3.1

1. Mercury, Venus
2. Saturn, Uranus (18)
3. Mercury
4. Pluto

5. Venus
6. Pluto
7. Jupiter
8. Pluto

9. Sun, Mercury, Venus, Earth, Mars, Jupiter, Saturn, Uranus, Neptune, Pluto

WORKSHEET 3.2

1. Alaska
2. Rhode Island
3. Mount McKinley, in Alaska

4. Death Valley, in California
5. Yellowstone National Park

6. Answers will vary
7. Answers will vary
8. Answers will vary

WORKSHEET 3.3

1. 1792
2. George Washington
3. An almanac records and predicts astronomical events (the rising and setting of the sun, for example), tides, weather, and other phenomena with respect to time.
4. a. Astronomical and weather predictions were more accurate.
   b. Advice was more useful.
   c. Its features were more entertaining.
5. Robert B. Thomas
6. A secret weather forecasting formula
7. 1861
8. Dropped weather forecasts by Roger Scaife

Almanac

The almanac is like a mini-library.

1. It is published every year.

2. It contains *current facts* and *statistics* on a wide range of subjects (governments, the arts, business, sports, and the weather).

3. Some of the information is in written reports, but much of it is shown in tables, charts, and graphs.

4. Most almanacs have an *index* that lists subjects in alphabetical order.

5. Almanacs often have *special features* such as "News of the Year in Pictures," timelines of important events in world history, and maps.

The originator of the first almanac in the United States was Dr. Benjamin Franklin of Philadelphia.

Two well-known almanacs are *The Information Please Almanac* and *The World Almanac and Book of Facts.*

TRANSPARENCY 3.1

Almanac Scavenger Hunt

(Resource: http://www.infoplease.com)

Directions: Divide the class into teams of two or three players.

Make sure each team has an online computer and/or a current almanac.

Teams locate and record the following information:

Weather for today _____

What happened ten years ago today _____

The biographical profile for today (students write the person's name and important dates [birth and death] and what the person is famous for)

_____

Almanac Research

Students use an almanac to do research on subjects that interest them or are part of the curriculum you are studying.

Directions:

1. Using the table of contents and the index of an almanac, write five or more questions on the lines below.
2. Write the answers to the questions on the next lines.
3. Cut the questions and answers apart.
4. Give the questions to the students and have them answer as quickly as they can. Be sure they include the page numbers on which they found their information. They can then check each other's answers using the answer sheets.
5. The winner is the student with the most correct answers in the shortest amount of time.

Variation

Students prepare the questions and answers, using the almanac, then exchange the questions among themselves and find the answers as quickly as they can.

Questions

1.-Q _____

2.-Q _____

3.-Q _____

4.-Q _____

5.-Q _____

Answers

1.-A _____

2.-A _____

3.-A _____

4.-A _____

5.-A _____

NAME _____   DATE _____

Planet Search

Directions: You are looking for quick information to compare the planets. Use the index and information of the almanac to answer the questions.

1. What planet has no moons?

2. What planet has the most moons?

3. What is the fastest orbiting planet?

4. What is the slowest orbiting planet?

5. What is the hottest planet?

6. What is the coldest planet?

7. What is the largest planet?

8. What is the smallest planet?

9. What is the order of the planets by orbit? Start with the sun.

   Sun,

States Search

Directions: You are studying the fifty states and would like to know geographical facts. Use the index and information of the almanac to answer the questions below.

1. Which state is the largest of the fifty states?

2. Which state is the smallest of the states?

3. What is the highest mountain in the United States and where is it located?

4. What is the lowest point in the United States and where is it located?

5. What is the oldest national park?

6. What is your state's motto?

7. When was your state admitted to the United States?

8. What is the origin of the name of your state?

Old Farmer's Almanac

(Resource: http://www.almanac.com/history/history.html)

Directions: Access the Internet almanac site to answer the following questions.

1. When was the first edition of the *Old Farmer's Almanac* published?

2. Who was president of the United States?

3. What by definition is an almanac?

4. What made this almanac better than the other almanacs of its time?

   a.

   b.

   c.

5. Who was the first editor of the *Old Farmer's Almanac?*

6. What did he use to make his almanac so much better than the rest?

7. What year did the almanac begin a heavy emphasis on farming?

8. What was the greatest of all almanac blunders?

Please . . . The Answer

Can you become a question writer for a quiz show? Here is your chance. You can also be a contestant and win a "million"— *compliments,* that is, for being so smart.

Directions:

Student Preparation

1. Explore the almanac to locate interesting information and facts.
2. First card: Use that information to write a question and correct answer.
3. Second card: Write the question, the correct answer, and two or three other logical choices for answers.

Librarian Preparation

1. Review and choose questions to use. The questions could be related to a social studies or science project.
2. Select teams.
3. State the game rules:

   a. The librarian will read the question and all the answer choices.

   b. Student team members will answer in rotation.

   c. The winning team is the one with the most correct answers.

Librarian Copy

Question _____

    A. _____

    B. _____

    C. _____

    D. _____

The correct answer is _____

Your name _____

Game Copy (Student View)

Question _____

    A. _____

    B. _____

    C. _____

    D. _____

Dictionary

To the Instructor

Dictionary skills are necessary. Students rely on spell checks in their word processing programs. Dictionaries are necessary for pronouncing words, learning word origins, and learning the parts of speech. There are specialized dictionaries for everything from art to zoology.

Objectives

1. Students learn how to locate words in a dictionary using guide words and entry words.

2. Students understand the purposes of a dictionary—spelling, definition, parts of speech, and pronunciation.

3. Students use the glossary of a textbook and compare it to a dictionary.

4. Students operate a "spell check" in a word processing program.

Materials ....

Transparencies

3.2 Dictionary ☐ ◧ ■

3.3 Singular to Plural ☐ ◧ ■

Dictionaries
Books containing glossaries
Computers

Teaching and Preparation ....

1. Demonstrate how to use the guide words at the top of a dictionary, encyclopedia, and glossary page.

2. Use transparencies to teach the following strategies:

   a. Decide how the word starts by saying it to yourself and identifying the beginning letter.

   b. Decide if the word will be in the front, middle, or back of the dictionary.

   c. Look at the guide words to find ones that you think have the same beginning three letters as the word you are trying to spell.

3. Review the pronunciation key and other parts of a dictionary entry.

4. Dictate sentences for students to type in a word processing program and check their spelling with the spell check function.

5. Review Internet references.

   http://www.dictionary.com

   http://www.askoxford.com (Ask Oxford.com)

   http://www.notam.uio.no/~hcholm/altlang/ (Alternative)

   http://www.onelook.com (Onelook Dictionary)

   http://www.yourdictionary.com/ (Yourdictionary.com)

Activity ....

3.3 Word of the Day ☐ ◧ ■

Worksheet ....

3.4 Dictionary Skills ☐

Games . . . .

3.2 Dictionary Word □ ◧ ■

3.3 Bluffo □ ◧ ■

Connections to the Curriculum . . . .

All curriculum areas use dictionary skills for introduction and understanding of topic vocabulary.

Answer Key . . . .

TRANSPARENCY 3.3

1. knives
2. monkeys
3. letters
4. sheep
5. lives
6. ladies
7. potatoes
8. sandwiches
9. feet
10. keys

WORKSHEET 3.4

A.

Set One

Body _5_   boast _3_   bobtail _4_   blush _2_   bond _6_   biology _1_

Set Two

Dress _4_   door _3_   donkey _2_   dull _6_   doggy _1_   drip _5_

B.

Set One

Bo/dy 2   boast 1   bob/tail 2   blush 1   bond 1   bi/ol/o/gy 4

Set Two

Dress 1   door 1   don/key 2   dull 1   dog/gy 2   drip 1

C. Answers may vary with dictionary used.

D.

Set One

Body N   boast V   bobtail N   blush V/ADJ   bond N/V   biology N

Set Two

Dress N/V   door N   donkey N   dull ADJ   doggy N   drip V

E. Answers may vary with dictionary used.

Dictionary

A dictionary lists words in alphabetical order and gives information about each word. All the words on a page are in alphabetical order between guide words.

Accent marks   Marks that show which syllable or syllables are stressed when saying a word.

Entry words   Bold words that are defined on a dictionary page. Entry words are listed in alphabetical order.

Etymology   History of a word [in brackets].

Guide words   Words located at the top of every page. They list the first and last entry words on a page. They help you know which words fall in alphabetical order between the entry words.

Illustrations   Pictures provided to make the definition clearer.

Parts of speech   Labels that tell you the different ways a word can be used.

Pronunciation key   Symbols to help pronounce the entry words.

Pronunciations   Phonetic respellings of a word.

Spelling and capital letters   Given for every entry word.

Syllable divisions   Breaks that show where to divide a word into syllables. Some dictionaries use heavy black dots to divide the syllables. Other dictionaries put an extra space between syllables.

Synonyms   Words with similar meanings. Antonyms (words with opposite meanings) may be listed last.

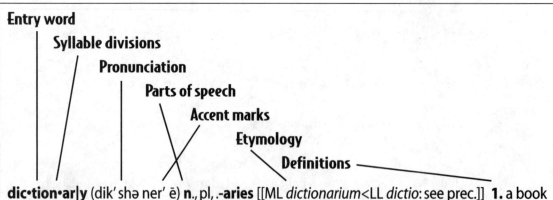

Entry word
    Syllable divisions
        Pronunciation
           Parts of speech
              Accent marks
                  Etymology
                      Definitions

dic•tion•ar|y (dik′ shə ner′ ē) **n.**, pl, **.-aries** [[ML *dictionarium*<LL *dictio*: see prec.]] **1.** a book of alphabetically listed words in a language, with definitions, etymologies, pronunciations, and other information; lexicon **2.** a book of alphabetically listed words in a language with their equivalents in another language [a Spanish-English dictionary] **3.** any alphabetically arranged list of articles relating to a special subject [a medical dictionary]

 **TRANSPARENCY 3.2**

Singular to Plural

Rules

A *singular* noun names one person, place, or thing. A *plural* noun names more than one person, place, or thing.

To form the **plural** of most nouns, **add s** at the end of the word.

Follow these rules for spelling other plural nouns:

es

Add **es** to nouns ending with **s, ss, x, z, ch,** and **sh.**

Change **y** to **i** and add **es** to nouns ending with a consonant and **y.**

Change **f** to **v** and add **es** for many nouns ending in **lf.**

s

Add **s** to nouns ending with a vowel and **y.**

Add **s** to nouns ending with a vowel and **o.**

Usually add **s** to nouns ending with a consonant and **o.**

Add **s** to all nouns ending in **ff** and some ending in **f** or **fe.**

Change the spelling of some irregular nouns.

Keep the spelling of some irregular nouns.

Directions: Use your dictionary to find the plurals of the following words.

1. knife _____
2. monkey_____
3. letter _____
4. sheep _____
5. life _____

6. lady _____
7. potato _____
8. sandwich _____
9. foot _____
10. key_____

Word of the Day

Directions:

1. Students will use a dictionary and write the definitions for new or difficult words they encounter in their daily lives.

2. Students will make cards to place on a word wall.

3. Students will keep a journal or notebook of new or unusual words.

4. Students will use the words to make a crossword or play hangman.

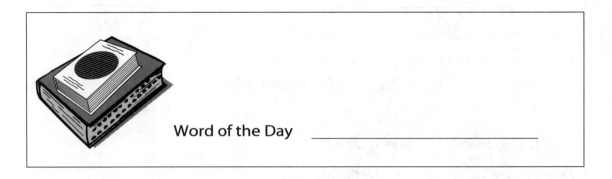

Word of the Day _____

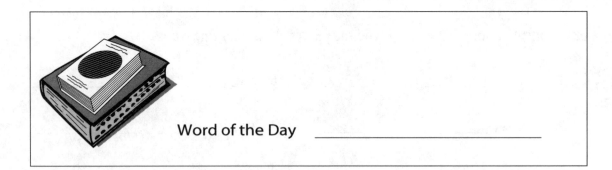

Word of the Day _____

NAME _____   DATE _____

Dictionary Skills

A. Alphabetize entry words

Place the following words in alphabetical order.

Set One

Body ____   boast ____   bobtail ____   blush ____   bond ____   biology ____

Set Two

Dress ____   door ____   donkey ____   dull ____   doggy ____   drip ____

B. Divide and conquer

Separate the words into syllables and write the number of syllables in each one.

C. Definitions

Write the definition of each of the words.

D. Word find

Write what part of speech each of the words is.

E. What word comes before and/or after each word?

Dictionary Word

Directions: Students use dictionaries to make 3 x 5 inch cards for the dictionary word game. The words used may be spelling lists, science vocabulary, or any other subject vocabulary words. The glossary of any book may also be used.

1. Card set one: Write the definition on side A and the word on side B.

2. Card set two: Keep side A blank and write the word on side B.

3. Card set three: Write the phonetic spelling on side A and the word on side B.

Set one: The students will see the *definition* side of the card and "guess" the word (definition to word).

OR

Set one: The students will see the *word* side and give the definition for the word (word to definition).

Set two: The students will see the blank side and the pronouncer will say the word for the student to spell (spelling bee style).

Set three: The students will see the phonetic spelling and pronounce the word and/or spell it correctly (students will use their skills of phonetic marks to spell the word or give the definition).

Rules

1. There are three boxes with a point value marked on the outside of the boxes. All boxes could have the same point value, or set one could be ten points for each correct answer, set two twenty points each, and set three thirty points for each correct answer.

2. Students are divided into two teams. The students in rotation pick a card from a box.

3. The student will give the definition, the word, or the correct spelling to earn points.

4. The team with the highest score wins.

Side A	Side B	
A book of alphabetically listed words with definitions, pronunciations, and other information	dictionary	Set One
	dictionary	Set Two
dik' shə ner' ē	dictionary	Set Three

Bluffo

The object of the game is to make other players think that you have the correct definition for a word on your card.

Directions: Some cards are blank. Readers make up a "bluff" to sound like a real definition.

1. There are three or four teams of students.

2. Prepare three or four cards for each "word" of the game, depending on the number of teams. Words may be from the student's spelling list or a subject vocabulary study.

3. Each round uses a card with the dictionary definition of a word plus two or three blank cards.

4. Hand a card to a reader from each team. The readers with blank cards must make up a definition for the word. The reader with the definition card reads that definition. (This works better if the reader tries to say the definition without actually reading.)

5. After the cards are "read," the librarian asks the teams to vote for the reader they thought had the real definition and the readers who were bluffing.

6. If the team selects the real definition they receive five points.

7. If a bluffer is selected as reading the real definition, the bluffer's team receives five points for each guess.

8. Guessing teams earn points by guessing the real definer; the bluffer's team earns points by other teams guessing them.

9. The winner is the team with the most points.

LESSON 3-C

Thesaurus

To the Instructor

Using a thesaurus can make students better readers and writers.

Objectives

1. Students learn how to locate synonyms and antonyms for selected words using a printed thesaurus.

2. Students learn how to find related and contrasted choices for selected words using a printed thesaurus.

3. Students use a word processing program and access the thesaurus tool to choose words to improve the vocabulary of their sentences.

Materials

Transparency

3.4 Thesaurus □ ◧ ■

Thesaurus books for the class
Computer with word processing for all students

Teaching and Preparation ....

1. Show how to access main entries in boldface type.

2. Demonstrate how to locate the synonyms and antonyms under each entry.

3. Explain how to locate the related and contrasted words.

4. Dictate sentences for students to type into a word processing program and check for synonyms or antonyms to improve or change the sentence.

5. Review Internet references.

   http://www.bartleby.com/62/ (Roget's II New Thesaurus)

   http://www.dictionary.com (Dictionary.com)

   http://www.wordsmyth.net (Wordsmyth)

   http://www.thesaurus.com (Thesaurus.com)

Activities ....

3.4 Thesaurus Team Chant □ ◫ ■

Students practice using spelling words or vocabulary from other subjects to create lists of synonyms and antonyms. (no page) □ ◫ ■

Worksheets ....

3.5 Building a Chain ◫ ■

3.6 Check Synonyms and Antonyms □ ◫ ■

Game ....

3.4 Build a Chain □ ◫ ■

Connections to the Curriculum ....

The Building a Chain worksheet words could be selected by any subject teacher. This is a good way to build a vocabulary in a subject area.

Dictionaries about specific subjects explain words and phrases related to subjects such as music and medicine.

Answer Key ....

WORKSHEET 3.5

Answers will vary.

WORKSHEET 3.6

Synonyms

1. envy, E
2. comedian, A
3. whiz, J
4. ailment, H

5. prevent, I
6. haunt, C
7. stretch, B

8. stir, F
9. bottleneck, D
10. distant, G

Antonyms

11. laugh, S
12. responsible, L
13. fortune, P
14. return, K

15. tarry, R
16. sanitary, M
17. grovel, Q

18. skeptic, O
19. handy, T
20. veer, N

Thesaurus

A thesaurus is a book of synonyms (words that have the same or nearly the same meaning).

Print Version

Entry word   Part of speech   Illustrative examples   Synonyms

Teach *v.*   Mr. LaFarge *teaches* French at the local high school. | The professor prefers to teach graduate students: give instruction in, conduct classes in, give lessons in, be employed as a teacher; give instruction to conduct class for, give lessons to instruct, educate, school, tutor, coach, drill, exercise, discipline, prepare, prime; inform, enlighten, edify, indoctrinate, inculcate, implant.

There were no antonyms given in this entry.

What are some antonyms you can think of?

Word Processor Version

Here is the information accessed through a word processing program when you select Tools, Thesaurus.

Looked up: Teach   Replace with synonym: Educate

Meanings:

    educate (v.)   educate

    educate in (v.)   tutor

    explain (v.)   school

                                 lecture

                                   instruct

                                   edify

                                 coach

                                 train

TRANSPARENCY 3.4

Thesaurus Team Chant

Directions:

Librarian or instructor provides a thesaurus for all groups.

Librarian or instructor discusses the need for rhyming, brevity, and meaning.

Students write and perform cheers and chants.

Students practice with peers.

Students perform on the intercom at events or from classroom to classroom.

Students use the thesaurus to discover synonyms and antonyms to elaborate words in the chant. Chants will be used to promote subjects, themes, or school events such as Library Week or holidays.

Example:

Synonym: winner = victor, champion, master, conqueror

Chant: Winners, winners, we are no beginners

Our team will be the victors, because we are good swimmers

Example:

Antonym: good = bad, evil, wicked, mean, cruel

Chant: We're bad, we're bad, we're going to make you sad

We play the game to win it all, but we won't be mean or small

NAME _____   DATE _____

Building a Chain

1. Use the thesaurus to locate the word in the first column.

2. Write a synonym, antonym, and related word for the entry.

3. Write a sentence for the each word, synonym, and antonym.

Word → **Synonym** → **Antonym** → **Related Word**

1.

2.

3.

4.

5.

NAME _____ DATE _____

Check Synonyms and Antonyms

You should try to make your written work interesting. Don't use the same word over and over. Use the thesaurus to find synonyms and antonyms for words you overuse.

Directions: Look for words in column B that are the synonyms or antonyms of the words in column A. Write the letter of the correct answer on the line that follows the words in Column A.

Synonyms are words that mean the same thing.

Antonyms are words that mean the opposite.

Synonyms

Column A		**Column B**
1. envy _____		A. humorist
2. comedian _____		B. extend
3. whiz _____		C. hangout
4. ailment _____		D. clog
5. prevent _____		E. jealous
6. haunt _____		F. energize
7. stretch _____		G. aloof
8. stir _____		H. illness
9. bottleneck _____		I. prohibit
10. distant _____		J. expert

Antonyms

Column A		**Column B**
11. laugh _____		K. depart
12. responsible _____		L. unreliable
13. fortune _____		M. dirty
14. return _____		N. make a beeline
15. tarry _____		O. believer
16. sanitary _____		P. poverty
17. grovel _____		Q. be proud
18. skeptic _____		R. hustle
19. handy _____		S. scowl
20. veer _____		T. all thumbs

Build a Chain

Word → **Definition** → **Synonym** → **Antonym** → **Sentence**

Directions:

1. The librarian or instructor develops a list of words. These words may be spelling words or subject words.

2. The librarian or instructor divides the class into teams.

3. The teams earn points by being able to add to the chain. A *chain* consists of the entry word, its definition, a synonym, an antonym, and a sentence using the entry word.

4. The librarian or instructor reads a word to two teams of players.

5. The first player of the first team gives the definition and earns one point; the second player a synonym and earns one point; the third an antonym and earns one point; and the fourth a sentence for the entry word and earns one point.

6. If a player can't keep the chain going, the other team can steal the points by giving the next correct answers.

7. The second team then tries to build a chain.

8. The team with the most points wins.

LESSON 3-D

Encyclopedia

To the Instructor

Encyclopedia skills are necessary for locating general information.

Objectives

1. Students learn how to use the index volume to locate information in encyclopedias.

2. Students compare using a specialized dictionary and multivolume and single volume encyclopedias.

3. Students compare electronic and print encyclopedias.

Materials

Transparency

3.5 Encyclopedia □ ◫ ■

Encyclopedias; multivolume and single volume
Specialized dictionaries
Electronic versions of encyclopedia

Teaching and Preparation ....

1. Demonstrate the use of the index volume of the encyclopedia set.

2. Explain how to locate a word in the dictionary and encyclopedia using guide words.

3. Access an electronic encyclopedia and dictionary and demonstrate similarities.

4. Review Internet references.

   http://www.eb.com

   http://www.encyclopedia.com

   http://education.yahoo.com/reference/encyclopedia (Britannica)

   http://www.bartleby.com/65/ (Columbia Encyclopedia)

   http://www.encyberpedia.com/ency.htm (Encyberpedia)

   http://www.si.edu/resource/faq/stact.htm (Encyclopedia.Smithsonian)

Worksheets ....

3.7 Encyclopedia ☐ ◫ ■

3.8 Dictionary and Encyclopedia ☐ ◫

Game ....

3.5 ENCYCLOPEDIA ☐ ◫ ■

Connections to the Curriculum ....

The librarian can have collaborating teachers supply topic questions (for example, about your state) for the students to research, connecting to all curriculum areas.

Science—plants, animals, volcanoes, weather

Social studies—historical sites, history, people, places, products, geography

Art—artists, masterpieces

Language—authors, literature

Music—musicians, famous works

Math—mathematicians

Any general information may be used in this lesson.

Answer Key ·

WORKSHEET 3.7

1. Suez Canal, S18
2. Truman, T19
3. Chile, C3
4. basketball, B2
5. football, F6
6. United States Constitution, U20
7. Kwanza, K11
8. Lincoln, L12
9. Statue of Liberty, S18
10. Liberty Bell, L12

WORKSHEET 3.8

1. Dictionary and encyclopedia
2. General multivolume; special single volume
3. Guide words give a clue as to what information would be included on the page on which they appear.
4. An encyclopedia is a general information starting point for research.
5. a. pronunciation
   b. spelling
   c. definition of words
6. Begin with the index volume.
7. To get current information; if you are missing volumes in an encyclopedia set
8. An index is a listing of topics and page numbers found in the encyclopedia set.
9. Special encyclopedias and dictionaries are limited to a single subject.

Encyclopedia

One section of the library is devoted to reference books. Reference books include encyclopedias, atlases, almanacs, indexes, dictionaries, thesauruses, and many other useful volumes. Most of these volumes do not circulate, for various reasons.

Encyclopedia

1. General information starting point.

2. Articles are arranged alphabetically by topic.

3. An index of topics (usually in the back of the last volume or in a separate volume) is available.

4. Related topics are listed at the end of most articles.

5. Different sets of encyclopedias may include different information.

6. Encyclopedias may be a single volume or as many as a volume for each letter of the alphabet plus an index volume.

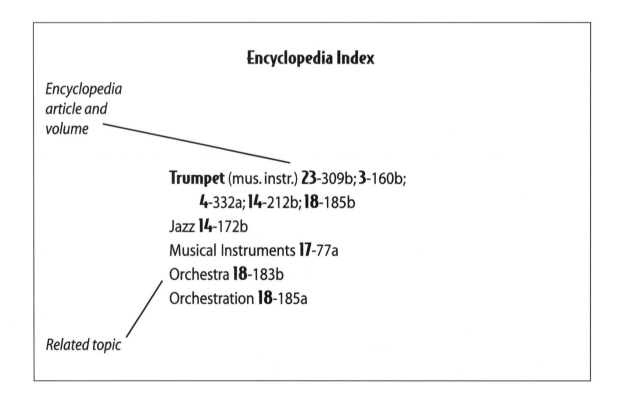

Encyclopedia Index

Encyclopedia article and volume

Trumpet (mus. instr.) **23**-309b; **3**-160b; **4**-332a; **14**-212b; **18**-185b
Jazz **14**-172b
Musical Instruments **17**-77a
Orchestra **18**-183b
Orchestration **18**-185a

Related topic

TRANSPARENCY 3.5

NAME _____   DATE _____

Encyclopedia

A	B	C	D	E	F	G	H	I	J	K	L	M	N	O	P – Q	R	S	T	U	V	W	X	Y	Z
1	2	3	4	5	6	7	8	9	10	11	12	13	14	15	16	17	18	19	20	21	22	23	24	25

Directions: Underline the key word in each question. Write the volume of the encyclopedia you would use to answer the question. (Students can also use the encyclopedia and answer the questions.)

1. Where is the Suez Canal located?

2. What is President Harry S. Truman's home state?

3. What is the capital of Chile?

4. What are the dimensions of a basketball court?

5. How many players are on a football team?

6. When was the Constitution of the United States signed?

7. How do you celebrate the holiday of Kwanza?

8. Who was the wife of Abraham Lincoln?

9. Who designed the Statue of Liberty?

10. Where is the Liberty Bell located?

Dictionary and Encyclopedia

Directions: Answer the following questions.

1. Which reference sources should you use when you begin a general search?

2. What are the two different styles of encyclopedias?

3. What is the purpose of guide words in an encyclopedia and dictionary?

4. What is an encyclopedia?

5. What are the three uses of a general dictionary?

    a.

    b.

    c.

6. Where is the best place to begin when you use an encyclopedia?

7. Why would you use an electronic encyclopedia?

8. What is the purpose of an index?

9. What are special encyclopedias and dictionaries?

ENCYCLOPEDIA

The object of the game is to use the encyclopedia for research. Students will find answers to questions the librarian has prepared.

Directions: *librarian or instructor*

1. Create a display board with twelve library pockets.

2. Place one of the letters of the word *encyclopedia* on each pocket.

3. Collaborate with the social studies and/or other subject teachers to develop questions the students will research in the encyclopedia. (The librarian can also use an index of a subject book or nonfiction book and develop questions.)

4. Place the related questions in the letter pockets.

5. Select letters based on the ability level and time allotment.

Directions: *students*

1. Select a letter pocket and research the question.

2. Locate the key word(s) and do research independently or in pairs or teams. The answers form clues to a common topic.

3. Students then pass on the research to their team, and together decide on the common subject. The teams earn points for correct answers and for being able to guess the common subject.

Example

E. How is *paper* made?

L. What is *hieroglyphics?*

P. Where did people use *cuneiform writing*?

O. Who is the inventor of the *newspaper*?

(Clues to guess common subject of *written communication*.)

GAME 3.5 cont.

E N C Y

C L O P

E D I A

LESSON 3-E

Record Books

To the Instructor

Record books are used to resolve arguments. They also identify strange facts. Humans have a natural curiosity to know the best, the biggest, and so on. Record books index and document phenomena.

Objectives

1. Students learn how to use fact books such as the *Guinness Book of Records* to locate information.

2. Students learn how to access the Internet and report an interesting fact to the class.

3. Students attempt to establish a record.

4. The librarian will publish a school or class "greatest" fact book to be in the library's circulation.

Materials . . . .

Transparency

3.6 Guinness and Other Record Books ☐ ◧ ■

Guinness Book of Records or any other fact books

Teaching and Preparation . . . .

1. Demonstrate record books as a reference tool using an index to locate information.
2. Compare various record books.
3. Review Internet references.

   http://www.guinnessworldrecords.com

   http://www.baseball-almanac.com

Activity . . . .

3.5 Our Record Book ☐ ◧ ■

Worksheet . . . .

3.9 Who Are the Record Holders? ☐ ◧ ■

Connections to the Curriculum . . . .

This is a great opportunity for the physical education department to collaborate with the library media center to produce and circulate a book of school records such as longest jump, most push-ups, etc.

Answer Key ....

WORKSHEET 3.9

1. Mount Everest, 29,078 feet, located in the Himalayans on the Tibet-Nepal border
2. Ostrich, 40 mph
3. Alaska, 591,004 square miles
4. Texas, 267,017 square miles
5. The most frequently used words in the English language are *the, of, and, to, a, in, that, is, I, it, for,* and *as.*
6. The most abundant element in the earth is iron.
7. Giraffe
8. Stegosaurus (plated lizard)
9. Valentina Vladimirova Tereshkova was the first woman to go into space, on June 16, 1963.
10. Answers may vary.

Guinness and Other Record Books

The *Guinness Book of Records* was first produced to assist in resolving arguments that might take place on matters of fact. The book is divided into the following sections: Earth and Space, Living World, Human Beings, Science and Technology, Buildings and Structures, Transport, Business World, Arts and Entertainment, Human Achievements, and Sports and Games.

Most prodigious eater The larva of the Polyphemus moth (Antheraea Polyphemus) of North America consumes an amount equal to 86,000 times its own birth weight in the first fifty-six days of its life. In human terms, this would be equivalent to a seven-pound baby taking in three hundred tons of nourishment!

Mammals • 61

Set a Record

If you wish to set a new record category for the *Guinness Book of Records,* then contact us (Guinness) and submit a brief proposal at least two months in advance of your attempt. This gives us (Guinness) a chance to say whether we (Guinness) think that your activity might have a chance of being included in future editions.

TRANSPARENCY 3.6

Our Record Book

Libraries in schools might and should have a section of books, poetry, or artwork created by the students. A record book of the accomplishments of a class or student might give incentives to other classes to outdo their sister's or brother's class. This section of the library is very interesting to parents and guardians, especially at open house times.

Directions: Students create a record book for your school. Each student who wishes to participate should fill out the following form. One or more students collect the entries and compile a record book. The teacher or librarian should serve as judge, and help keep activities safe.

1. I would like to try for the record of _____

2. I know I must be able to accomplish my attempts in one class period.

3. I know my skill must be safe for me, others, and the entire school.

4. I know that the judge's decisions, rules, and qualifications are final, and I can't argue with him or her.

5. I know that the record information will be placed in the *Record Book* for the class and/or school for others to see and challenge.

6. I will supply the following materials needed for my record attempt

   _____

7. I would like to try on (date) _____

Name _____

Grade/Home room _____

Who Are the Record Holders?

Directions: Use a copy of the *Guinness Book of Records* to discover who these record holders are.

1. What is the highest mountain?

2. What is the fastest bird on land?

3. What is the largest state in the United States?

4. What is the largest state in the *contiguous* United States?

5. What are the most common words in the English language?

6. What is the most abundant element in the earth?

7. What is the tallest land animal?

8. What is the most brainless animal that roamed the earth?

9. Who was the first woman in space?

10. (Add questions about sports persons, team and individual records, or current topics of study: Who or what is the fastest, slowest, most, biggest, and so on.)

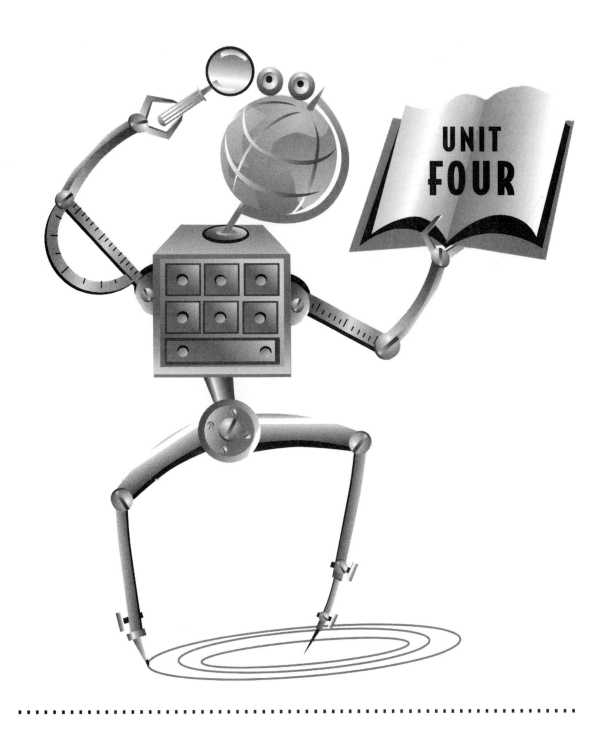

Using Reference Resources:
Geography

LESSON 4-A

Atlas

To the Instructor

A printed atlas has definite advantages over an online atlas. Online maps are often small and hard to read, lack an index, are slow to download, and are not always in color when printed. Printed atlases are portable and have indexes and other information besides maps.

Objectives

1. Students learn how to use the contents and index pages of an atlas to locate cities, states, and so on.

2. Students learn the terms *compass rose, latitude, longitude, scale, legend, coordinates,* and *grid lines*.

Materials

Transparency

4.1 Atlas Glossary ☐ ◧ ■

Atlases for each student

Teaching and Preparation ....

1. Demonstrate how to use the contents and index pages of an atlas to find information about cities, countries, and so on.

2. Define geographic terms.

3. Explain the use of a *compass rose, legend,* and *scale* for map information.

4. Use *latitude* and *longitude* as *coordinate points.*

5. Access an electronic atlas and compare the advantages and disadvantages of a printed atlas versus an electronic atlas.

6. Review Internet references.

   http://education.yahoo.com/reference/factbook/

   http://www.lib.utexas.edu/maps

   http://www.lib.washington.edu/Subject/Maps

   http://www.atlapedia.com (Atlapedia Online)

   http://www.worldatlas.com/aatlas/world.htm (World Atlas of Maps, Flags, & Geography Facts)

   http://www.atlas-games.com (Atlas Games)

Worksheets ....

4.1 Virtual Vacation □ ◧ ■

4.2 Atlas, Atlas, Atlas ■

4.3 Hop, Skip, and Jump! □ ◧

Games ....

4.1 Passport Hop, Skip, and Jump! □ ◧ ■

Software: Play the *Where in the World Is Carmen SanDiego?* software games to reinforce geography skills. (no page) □ ◧ ■

Connections to the Curriculum ....

Atlas searches begin with the index. Knowing how to use indexes in textbooks and reference books is the first step in locating the map that will answer the question of where something is.

Answer Key ....

WORKSHEET 4.1

Answers will vary.

WORKSHEET 4.2

Destination	Location
Alexandria, Egypt	31°N 30°E
Amazon River	2°S 53°W
Beijing, China	40°N 116°E
Berlin, Germany	52°N 13°E
Bombay, India	19°N 73°E
Buenos Aires, Argentina	34°S 58°W
London, England	51°N 0.07°W
Montreal, Canada	45°N 73°W
Rio de Janeiro, Brazil	22°S 43°W
Tennessee River, U. S.	36°N 88°W
Tigris River, Asia	35°N 44°E
Cape Town, South Africa	33°S 18°E
Athens, Greece	38°N 23°E
Denmark	56°N 8°E
Jerusalem, Israel	31°N 35°E
Arctic Ocean	85°N 170°E
Cuba	22°N 79°W
Japan	36°N 133°E
Luxembourg, Belgium	49°N 6°E
Persian Gulf	28°N 51°E
Timbuktu, Mali	17°N 3°W
Saudi Arabia	22°N 46°W
Vera Cruz, Mexico	19°N 96°W
Rome, Italy	42°N 13°E
Sydney, Australia	34°S 151°E
Mississippi River	32°N 91°W
Mediterranean Sea	36°N 13°E
Nile River	28°N 31°E
Yangtze River	31°N 117°E
Santo Domingo, Dominican Republic	18°N 70°W
Chile, South America	35°S 72°W

WORKSHEET 4.3

1. Imaginary grid lines are on maps to help with location of cities, countries, and so on.
2. A compass rose is a drawing showing north, south, east, and west directions.
3. A legend explains the pictures and symbols shown on a map.
4. Scale is a sample ruler showing that one inch or centimeter equals real mileage or kilometers.
5. North, south, east, and west
6. Begin searches with the index or table of contents of the atlas.
7. Latitude is imaginary lines around the earth running east to west.
8. Longitude is imaginary lines around the earth running north to south.
9. Advantages: many people can access at the same time; information is up to date.
10. Disadvantages: images are small and hard to read; images don't print in color and are slow to download; there is no index or scale.

Atlas Glossary

Compass rose A representation of directions placed on maps.

Equator An imaginary circle around the earth dividing the earth into two hemispheres.

Grid lines A network of evenly spaced horizontal and vertical lines for locating points when placed over a map.

International Date Line An imaginary line drawn north and south through the Pacific Ocean, largely along the 180th meridian. This is where each calendar day begins at midnight. When it is Sunday just west of the line, it is Saturday just east of it.

Latitude Points north and south of the equator measured from the equator by imaginary lines on the earth drawn left to right.

Longitude A series of imaginary lines drawn from the North Pole to the South Pole, called meridians, that measure eastward or westward from the prime meridian that runs through Greenwich, England.

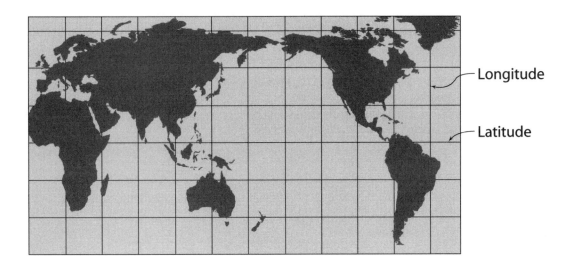

TRANSPARENCY 4.1

Legend   A key, such as to land use or major minerals, that accompanies a map.

```
┌─────────────────────────────────────┐
│               LEGEND                 │
│                                      │
│   Mountains   ^^^                    │
│                                      │
│   Cities      •                      │
│                                      │
│   Capital City    ✳                  │
│                                      │
│   Forest      ▲ ▲ ▲                  │
│                                      │
│   Border ___··___··___··___          │
│                                      │
│   One Inch = Five Miles              │
└─────────────────────────────────────┘
```

Meridians   Vertical lines that stretch from the North to the South poles and measure longitude 0 to 180 degrees east and west.

Parallels   Horizontal lines that circle the globe parallel to the equator and measure latitude 0 to 90 degrees north and south.

Prime Meridian   The line of longitude that is measured both east and west; 0 degrees longitude. It passes through Greenwich, England.

Scale Information on a map that one inch or centimeter is equal to a number of miles or kilometers in the real world. (The proportion that a map bears to the area that it represents.)

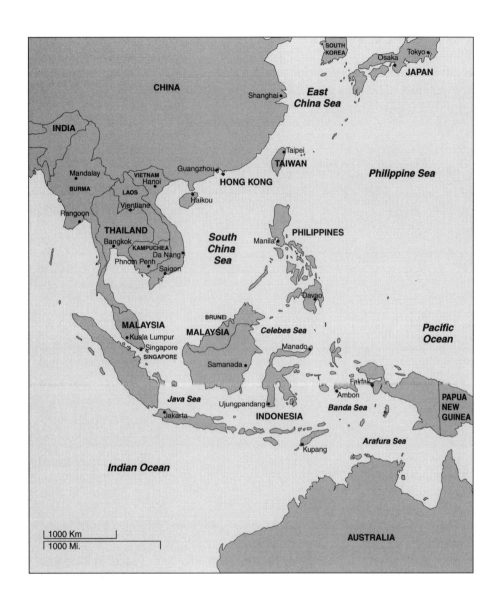

NAME _____   DATE _____

Virtual Vacation

Where would you like to go on a vacation? Plan the trip. Use the atlas and other reference materials available in your library.

Starting point (city/state)	Transportation (plane, train, car) (approximate miles)	Destination (family heritage, landmarks, amusement park) (city, state, country)
1.		(to another city in your state)
2.		(to another state)
3.		(to another country)
Use a map and draw a circle around your city starting point.	Draw a line from the starting point to your destination.	Place an X on your destination point.

Use the *legend* of your maps to calculate the number of miles to your destination.

How many miles from your starting point to destination?

NAME _____ DATE _____

Atlas, Atlas, Atlas

Directions: Use your print or electronic atlas and write the latitude and longitude of the following locations.

Destination	Location
Alexandria, Egypt	
Amazon River	
Beijing, China	
Berlin, Germany	
Bombay, India	
Buenos Aires, Argentina	
London, England	
Montreal, Canada	
Rio de Janeiro, Brazil	
Tennessee River, U.S.	
Tigris River, Asia	
Cape Town, South Africa	
Athens, Greece	
Denmark	
Jerusalem, Israel	
Arctic Ocean	
Cuba	
Japan	
Luxembourg, Belgium	
Persian Gulf	
Timbuktu, Mali	
Saudi Arabia	
Vera Cruz, Mexico	
Rome, Italy	
Sydney, Australia	
Mississippi River	
Mediterranean Sea	
Nile River	
Yangtze River	
Santo Domingo, Dominican Republic	
Chile, South America	

Hop, Skip, and Jump!

NAME _____ DATE _____

1. Why are there imaginary grid lines on maps and globes?

2. What is a compass rose?

3. What is a legend?

4. What is "scale"?

5. What are the four directions on every map?

6. Where is the starting point for every atlas search?

7. What is latitude?

8. What is longitude?

9. What are some advantages of using an electronic atlas?

10. What are some disadvantages of using an electronic atlas?

Passport Hop, Skip, and Jump!

Directions:

1. Students are divided into teams. Each team has two players.

2. Provide students with names of cities, countries, rivers, and so on. Choose locations from newspaper headlines or current events.

3. Students use atlases to "visit" or find the location of each name. Teams "visit" locations *in order.* Teams use latitude, longitude, or grid coordinates for answers. The answers are written on the lines of their passport.

4. Passports will be stamped to prove the teams have been to the locations.

Alternative: Students can play the *Where in the World Is Carmen SanDiego?* or *Where in the USA Is Carmen SanDiego?* software games.

Destination	Location

. . . . **GAME 4.1 cont.**

Passport

Name(s)

1. _____

2. _____

3. _____

4. _____

5. _____

6. _____

7. _____

8. _____

9. _____

10. _____

142

LESSON 4-B

Maps

To the Instructor

Maps are located in the library media center's vertical file, and in atlases, encyclopedias, and various other books.

Objectives

1. Students gain knowledge of various map and geography terms.
2. Students become skilled in using various print and electronic maps.

Materials

Transparency

    4.2 Map Glossary ☐ ◧ ■

Maps
Online maps
Current newspapers

Teaching and Preparation . . . .

1. Display and discuss various maps and their purposes.

2. Access online map sites and discuss their advantages and disadvantages.

3. Review Internet references.

   http://www.geographynetwork.com/ (Geography Network)

   http://fermi.jhuapl.edu/states/about.html (state maps)

   http://www.maps.com/

   http://www.teachervision.com/lesson-plans/lesson-60.html (puzzles)

   http://www.teachervision.com/lesson-plans/lesson-6642.html

   http://www.teachervision.com/lesson-plans/lesson-49.html

Activities . . . .

4.1 Weather Map □ ◪ ■

4.2 Maps in the News □ ◪ ■

Worksheets . . . .

4.4 Check Map Terms □ ◪

4.5 My Land Map □

4.6 Home Team Advantage □ ◪ ■

Game . . . .

4.2 Orienteering in the Library Media Center □ ◪ ■

Connections to the Curriculum . . . .

Art—color or make symbols for maps; create personal maps of rooms, and so on

Language arts—practice writing and giving directions to locations

Math—research the costs of cruises

Science—weather locations

Social studies—history, travel, current event locations

Answer Key ....

ACTIVITIES 4.1 AND 4.2

Answers will vary

WORKSHEET 4.4

1. Historical map
2. Legend
3. Equator
4. Compass rose
5. A section of the earth after it is divided into halves: northern, southern, eastern, and western
6. Economic map
7. Mercator projection
8. Navigational map
9. Latitude
10. North, south, east, and west

WORKSHEET 4.5

1. Lucky Town
2. Richman

3. Kitchen
4. Lucky Town

5. No
6. A scale marker

WORKSHEET 4.6

WORKSHEET 4.6 cont.

Name of Team	Home Town of the Team (city and state)
1. St. Louis Cardinals	St. Louis, Missouri
2. New York Yankees	New York, New York
3. Chicago Bears	Chicago, Illinois
4. San Francisco 49ers	San Francisco, California
5. Jacksonville Jaguars	Jacksonville, Florida
6. Denver Broncos	Denver, Colorado
7. Texas Rangers	Arlington, Texas
8. Minnesota Twins	Minneapolis, Minnesota
9. Tennessee Titans	Nashville, Tennessee
10. New England Patriots	Foxborough, Massachusetts
11. Dallas Cowboys	Dallas, Texas
12. Atlanta Falcons	Atlanta, Georgia
13. Seattle Mariners	Seattle, Washington
14. Pittsburgh Pirates	Pittsburgh, Pennsylvania
15. Washington Redskins	Washington, D.C.
16. Carolina Panthers	Charlotte, North Carolina
17. Miami Dolphins	Miami, Florida
18. Boston Red Sox	Boston, Massachusetts
19. Minnesota Vikings	Minneapolis, Minnesota
20. California Angels	Anaheim, California

Map Glossary

Cartographer   A person whose job is making maps.

Climate map   Contains graphics that show marine, highland, desert, tropical rain forest, Mediterranean average weather.

Compass rose   A direction finder showing the four cardinal directions: north, south, east, and west.

Culture map   A map that gives information about the way people live.

Economic map   A map that depicts the area's economy with pictures or charts.

Elevation map   A map that shows the height of mountains, plains, and other landforms.

Equator   Imaginary line that circles the earth at 0 degrees latitude, dividing the earth into northern and southern hemispheres.

Geography   A field of study that deals with the surface of the earth, or the physical surface features of a region or area.

Grid lines   A system of imaginary lines called meridians and parallels that measure locations in degrees.

Hemisphere   A section of the earth after it is divided into halves: northern, southern, eastern, and western.

Historical map   A map that gives information about a place in the past, or a place's change over time.

International Date Line   The meridian opposite the prime meridian that measures 180 degrees longitude and marks the change in the calendar day.

Latitude   East to west lines drawn on a map or globe.

Legend   A key that identifies and explains symbols on the map.

Longitude   North to south lines drawn on a map or globe.

 **TRANSPARENCY 4.2**

Map projections   Different pictures of the earth drawn by a cartographer.

Equal-area projection divides the earth into equal areas. Distorts near the edges of the map.

Mercator projection gives an accurate view near the equator, but land near the poles is distorted.

Polar projection uses as its center either the North Pole or the South Pole.

Meridians   Vertical lines that stretch from the north to the south and measure longitude 0 to 180 degrees east and west.

Navigational map   A map used by sailors or pilots to get to their destinations.

Parallels   Horizontal lines that circle the globe parallel to the equator and measure latitude 0 to 90 degrees north and south.

Physical map   A map with a legend that shows graphics to depict plains, deserts, mountains, oceans, rivers, and so on.

Political map   A map that shows the boundaries of countries. Stars or other symbols would show capitals and large cities.

Population map   A map that shows how many people live in an area.

Prime meridian   The meridian at Greenwich, England, that measures 0 degrees longitude and divides east and west longitude.

Scale   A marker that describes how real distance on the earth is represented by the distances shown on the map.

Story map   A map that tells a story as a sequence of events.

Topographic map   A map that shows landforms.

Weather Map

Directions:

1. Students check the weather map in today's newspaper, and look specifically for the following:

   Find areas that had severe weather: showers, snow, sun, and so on.

   Locate your home city on the weather map.

   Chart the weather for your area for a week.

   Predict the weather for your area for a week.

2. Students draw a weather map of their area that shows the isobars and a weather prediction.

3. Discuss how maps such as this can help us prepare for weather emergencies.

Maps in the News

Directions: Maps are not only in atlases and other books containing maps. They can also be found in the newspaper and in magazines. Students use the local newspaper to find or answer the following:

1. Locate all the maps in today's newspaper.

2. Name the cities, states, or countries for these maps.

3. Write the pages where you find the maps.

4. Locate the same maps in the library's atlases.

5. How are the maps the same, and how are they different?

6. Locate a story with an *international* dateline and list the city and country.

7. Locate a story with a *national* dateline and list the city and state.

8. Locate a story for your state and list the date.

9. Are there maps for these stories? If not, locate a map in your atlas.

NAME _____ DATE _____

Check Map Terms

Directions: Use an atlas to answer the following questions.

1. What kind of map shows information about a place's past, or a place's change over time?

2. What is used to explain and identify symbols used on the map?

3. What is the line that circles the earth at 0 degrees latitude, dividing the earth?

4. What is used as a direction finder showing the four cardinal directions?

5. What is a hemisphere?

6. Which map would you use to tell about an area's economy?

7. Which map projection gives an accurate view near the equator?

8. What kind of map would a pilot or sailor use?

9. Is the equator an example of a latitude or longitude line?

10. What are the four cardinal directions?

My Land Map

• **Kitchen**   * **Lucky Town**

      Ranch •

• **Hill City**

                              • **Fox Land**

            • **Richman**

N

S

1. What city is east of Fox Land?

2. What city is southwest of Fox Land?

3. What city is north of Ranch?

4. Which city is the capital?

5. Does this map show you the distances between cities?

6. What do you need in the legend to show distances?

NAME _____   DATE _____

Home Team Advantage

Directions: Where do these sports teams call home? Use an outline map of the United States, an atlas, and/or an almanac to locate the "homes" of these sports teams. Fill in the chart below.

Name of Team	Home Town of the Team (city and state)
1. St. Louis Cardinals	
2. New York Yankees	
3. Chicago Bears	
4. San Francisco 49ers	
5. Jacksonville Jaguars	
6. Denver Broncos	
7. Texas Rangers	
8. Minnesota Twins	
9. Tennessee Titans	
10. New England Patriots	
11. Dallas Cowboys	
12. Atlanta Falcons	
13. Seattle Mariners	
14. Pittsburgh Pirates	
15. Washington Redskins	
16. Carolina Panthers	
17. Miami Dolphins	
18. Boston Red Sox	
19. Minnesota Vikings	
20. California Angels	

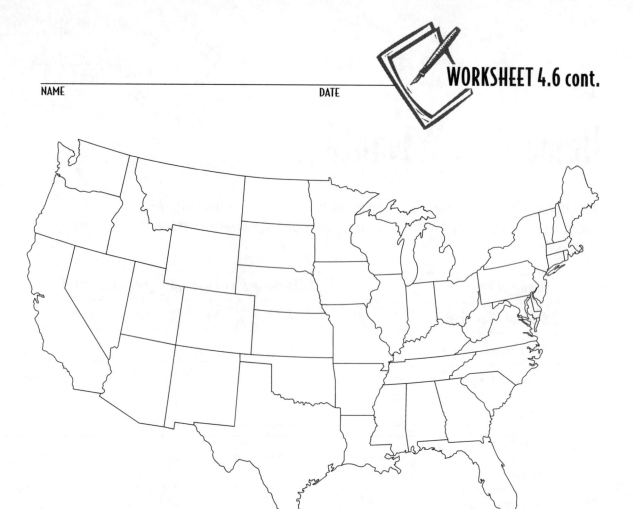

Directions: Use the list of sports teams and your atlas. Place a dot in the correct location of the hometown of each team. Write the number of the team next to the dot.

1. San Francisco Giants	12. San Francisco 49ers	22. St. Louis Cardinals
2. Indianapolis Colts	13. Atlanta Falcons	23. Buffalo Bills
3. Florida Marlins	14. Detroit Lions	24. Philadelphia Eagles
4. Seattle Mariners	15. Chicago Bears	25. Kansas City Chiefs
5. St. Louis Rams	16. New Orleans Saints	26. California Angels
6. Denver Broncos	17. Los Angeles Dodgers	27. Jacksonville Jaguars
7. Oakland A's	18. Washington Redskins	28. Minnesota Vikings
8. Baltimore Ravens	19. Pittsburgh Pirates	29. Dallas Cowboys
9. Colorado Rockies	20. Baltimore Orioles	30. Texas Rangers
10. New York Giants	21. Minnesota Twins	31. Pittsburgh Steelers
11. Carolina Panthers		

Orienteering in the Library Media Center

Directions:

1. Students and/or instructors will need setup time. One class or team can make the tasks for another class or team.

2. Draw the floor plan of your library media center or direction cards. Incorporate areas of the library media center that you would like the students to become more acquainted with.

3. Choose a class or team to direct the other team around the library using clues or instructions.

4. Students will use the Internet, computers, display cases, tables, and the circulation desk as parts of the trek.

5. Make it a treasure hunt by having a reward at the end of the trek.

Examples of clues:

- Go north 40 paces.
- Open the red book on the shelf with a green tag.
- Start at the biography section. Open the book about our governor. Follow the directions.

LESSON 4-C

Gazetteer: A Geographical Dictionary

To the Instructor ....

The Gazetteer is one of the "special, dedicated" dictionaries available in the reference section of the library media center.

Objectives ....

1. Students gain knowledge of specialized dictionaries and particularly the geographical dictionary.

2. Students learn how to use a Gazetteer to locate political and physical features of the earth.

Materials ....

Transparencies

    4.3 Gazetteer Glossary □ ◧ ■

    4.4 Geography and Earth Facts □ ◧ ■

Specialized dictionaries (language, computer, and so on)
A geographical dictionary (Gazetteer)

Teaching and Preparation ....

1. Demonstrate how to locate information using a Gazetteer.

2. Display geographical terms and symbols found in the Gazetteer, map legend, and map for the students to practice finding resources, rivers, and mountains.

3. Scroll down the Gazetteer selections for the areas of the world you are studying.

4. Review Internet references.

   http://www.lib.utexas.edu/maps (Glossary of Cartographic terms)

   http://www.bartleby.com/eby.com/69/ (Columbia Gazetteer of North America)

   http://www.gazetteer.de/ (The World Gazetteer)

   http://www.gazeteer.com (Worldwide Gazetteer)

Worksheet ....

4.7 Where in the World? ■

Game ....

4.3 Pin the World ■

Connections to the Curriculum ....

Social studies—collaborate map skills and Gazetteer all year long

Answer Key ....

WORKSHEET 4.7

1. Geographical dictionary
2. Reference section
3. No. They are expensive and usually the library purchases one every several years.
4. No. Gazetteers are purchased every four or five years.
5. Pronunciations, definitions, location, history, maps, population, size
6. True
7. Anyone who wants pronunciations, histories, locations, and so on without the use of an atlas, map, or book about a country.

Gazetteer Glossary

Cross-references   References to related articles that may be found within the body of the article.

Detail information in entry   Geographical location, rank in area and the area, rank in population and the population, capital nickname, flower, motto, chief products, chief cities, political divisions.

Entry information   Locations, area and population, geographical and physical features, economic data, items of general interest, and historical information.

Entry word   Bold-faced words in alphabetical order, with syllabic divisions, pronunciations, and alternative forms. Some entries are accompanied by maps, tables, and/or charts.

Gazetteer   A special dictionary of geography words such as cities, countries, continents, waterways, and so on.

Natural features   Physical features, such as lengths of rivers, heights of mountains, lengths and areas of islands and lakes; economic data, such as navigability of rivers, mineral wealth of mountains, wealth of agricultural and industrial products; date of discovery, colonization, or acquisition.

Name of country, river, city

Pronunciation

Definition, location, population, size

History

Maps

See, See also, See table

 **TRANSPARENCY 4.3**

Geography and Earth Facts

Geography Facts

Amazon Rain Forest (South America) is the **largest tropical rain forest** in the world.

Andes Mountains (South America) are the **longest mountain range** on earth.

Angel Falls (South America) is the **highest waterfall** in the world.

Arica (Chile) has the **least rain** of any place on earth.

Dead Sea shore (Asia) is the **lowest point** on land in the world.

Great Barrier Reef (coast of Australia) is the **largest group of coral reefs** in the world.

Greenland (North America) is the **largest island** in the world.

Lake Superior (North America) is the **largest freshwater lake** in the world.

Mariana Trench, Challenger Deep, (Pacific Ocean) is the **deepest point** in the ocean.

Mount Everest (Asia) is the **highest mountain** in the world.

Mount Waialeale (Kauai, Hawaii) is the **rainiest place** on earth.

Nile River (Africa) is the **longest river** in the world.

Sahara Desert (Africa) is the **largest desert** on earth.

Earth Facts

Age: four billion, six hundred million years old

Weight: 6.6 sextillion tons

Equatorial circumference: 24,859-82/100 miles

NAME _____   DATE _____   **WORKSHEET 4.7**

Where in the World?

Directions: Answer the following questions about the Gazetteer.

1. What is another name for a Gazetteer?

2. Where are the Gazetteers located in the library media center?

3. May the Gazetteers be "borrowed" or taken out of the library media center? Why or why not?

4. Can you find up-to-date information about population in a Gazetteer? Why or why not?

5. What kind of information can be found in a Gazetteer?

6. True or false: A Gazetteer is a dictionary or index of geographical names.

7. Who needs the information found in a Gazetteer?

160

Pin the World

Directions: The object of the game is to use a Gazetteer and map to locate cities, rivers, mountains, and so on that are in the news or are part of a social studies lesson collaboration.

1. Students are divided into teams. (Each team should have access to a Gazetteer or the online Gazetteers site.)

2. The librarian reads the name of the geographical feature and writes it on a display board so that the students will know the correct spelling.

3. Students use the Gazetteer to access information about the geographical feature.

4. Students use the information to go to a large map of the world, country, or state the students are studying and "pinpoint" the location.

5. The team receives points for being the first to correctly "pin" the location. It works better with two identical maps, so that the students don't "fight" to see where to place their pin.

"Pins" can be actual pins placed into a map on a cork board. Alternatively, pins can be made by copying, cutting out, and laminating the "pin" pictured on this page. Duplicate as many "pins" as you need. When cutting, do not cut out around the pin itself. Cut a larger square area of paper around the "pin."

Attach the "pin" to the map by using a removable glue stick, or removable sticky tack.

Using Reference Resources:
Biography and Quotations

LESSON 5-A

Biography

To the Instructor

There are three kinds of biographies: *biography* (about one person, written by another or others), *autobiography* (written by the person about him- or herself), and *collective biography* (about groups of related people).

Objectives

1. Students read and learn about biography, autobiography, collective biography books, biographical dictionaries, memoirs, and other related materials.

2. Students learn how to write biographies, or autobiographies.

3. Students understand that historical fiction, movies, and videos are not always accurate biography information.

Materials

Transparencies

5.1 Types of Biography ☐ ◨ ■

5.2 Memoir ☐ ◨ ■

Displays of different biographical materials
Encyclopedias
A video biography of someone like Helen Keller
Historical fiction books

Teaching and Preparation ....

1. Demonstrate the various biographical materials in your library.

2. List the expected information for a good biography.

3. Compare historical fiction books with a true biography about a famous person.

4. Connect spine labels (92, B, and 920) with the different kinds of biographies.

5. Review Internet references.

   http://www.s9.com

   http://www.biography.com

   http://amillionlives.com

   http://go.to/realnames (Real people's names)

   http://www.neosoft.com/~davo/livedead/ (Who's alive and who's dead)

   http://blackhistory.eb.com (Encyclopaedia Britannica's guide to black history)

   http://frank.mtsu.edu/~kmiddlet/history/women.html (American women's history)

Activities ....

5.1 Take Notes: Personal Interviews ☐ ◪ ■

5.2 Take Notes: Print Biographies ☐ ◪ ■

5.3 Take Notes: Outline ☐ ◪ ■

5.4 Interview Show ◪ ■

5.5 Family Biography ☐ ◪ ■

5.6 You're Special ☐ ◪ ■

5.7 Biography Trading Cards ◪ ■

5.8 Picture Collage ☐ ◪ ■

5.9 Secret Identity ☐ ◪ ■

5.10 Cartoon Biography ☐ ◪ ■

Worksheet ....

5.1 Biographies ☐

Game ....

5.1 Biography Jeopardy ☐ ◻ ◼

Connections to the Curriculum ....

The social studies teacher will collaborate with the librarian and a computer specialist to research a famous black American during Black History Month or a famous woman during Women's History Month, and so on.

Answer Key ....

WORKSHEET 5.1

1. A biography is a book or story about a person's life written by a different person who has studied documents or interviewed people who knew the subject to tell an accurate account of the events of the subject's life in chronological order.
2. An autobiography is a book or story about a person's life written by the person him- or herself.
3. A collective biography is a book or story about lives of people who are grouped together by some common thread such as a sport, an occupation, or some similar subject.
4. A biography spine label shows the first three letters of the biography subject and a B, 92, or 920, depending on the library's choice.
5. Biographies are alphabetized on the shelves by the subject's last name. The collective biographies may be in the nonfiction Dewey sections, first by the number 920 and then by the subject's last name.
6. 920
7. No. Historical fiction has a base in history but emphasizes exciting or embellished events.
8. It is a large, single-source volume of short biographies of famous people who have staying value and made an impact on history.
9. The biographical dictionary is an expensive, heavy, and often outdated book of people that elementary school students may not be interested in.
10. The Internet is updated daily. Current celebrities, candidates, and the like are written about as events occur. The question is to the accuracy of each entry.

Types of Biography

A **biography** is the story of someone's life written by another person.

An **autobiography** is writing about one's own life.

A **collective biography** is the story of a group of people's lives tied together by their profession, family, or history.

The **biographical dictionary** has short, concise entries about famous people.

Biographies are the easiest materials to find in the library because the researcher looks for the person's last name in the biography section of the library media center.

The spine of the book may have a **B** for "biography" above the first three letters of the person's name. A **92** above the first three letters of the person's name is used in some libraries.

Libraries use the **920** Dewey Decimal Classification System section of the library for collective biographies in print.

Libraries have biography videos, but care should be taken to ensure their accuracy.

The Internet is another source of information. A good biographical search site is http://www.s9.com.

It is recommended that you find at least three sources of information about your biographical subject to confirm and collate the stories and important dates.

Memoir

As a **biography**—it is the life of a person written by someone who knew the subject well.

As an **autobiography**—it is an objective telling of the life of a person written to emphasize the outward events rather than being inward and subjective.

As a **report or record**—it is the important events of a person's life based on the writer's personal observation or knowledge.

A **memoir** can be developed through journals, letters, diaries, or any personal writings.

Memoirs are recollections of a person's life plus embellishments by the biographer for interest and are not always accurate to historical events.

To write a report about a memoir biography, the student may obtain the information from diaries or collect it firsthand through personal interviews.

 **TRANSPARENCY 5.2**

Take Notes: Personal Interviews

Directions: Students can use this form to gather information for a biography of someone they know. After completing the form, they will rate the information below and write a short paragraph about the person.

Name of person interviewed_____

Place of interview_____

Permission for recording granted—y/n _____

Tape recorder used for interview—y/n _____

Video camera used for interview—y/n _____

Phone interview—y/n _____

Mail interview—y/n _____

Address_____

Date of interview _____

Thank-you note sent—y/n _____

Copy of finished product sent to person—y/n _____

Questions to be used for interview (develop on a separate sheet of paper)

Rate information for usefulness

Exactly what I needed—y/n _____   Didn't provide enough detail—y/n _____

Answered partially—y/n _____   Right questions asked—y/n _____

Wasn't on right topic—y/n _____   Questions answered to satisfaction—y/n _____

Too hard to understand—y/n _____   Good start—y/n _____

My Notes

Take Notes: Print Biographies

Directions: Students can use this form to gather information for a biography of a famous person and compare information with another student. After completing the form, they will rate the information below and write a short paragraph about the person.

Name of biography person _____

Author _____

Title _____

Publisher—city—copyright date _____

Number of pages _____

Table of contents—y/n _____

Chapters—y/n _____

How many chapters? _____

Index—y/n _____

Glossary—y/n _____

Graphics—y/n _____

Rate information for usefulness

Exactly what I needed—y/n _____   Didn't provide enough detail—y/n _____

Answered partially—y/n _____   Out of date—y/n _____

Wasn't on right topic—y/n _____   Good start—y/n _____

Too hard to understand—y/n _____

My Notes

Take Notes: Outline

Directions: Students can use this form to gather information for a biography of a famous person and compare information with another student. After completing the form, they will write a short paragraph about the person.

Name of person _____

Childhood information _____

    Date of birth_____

    Place of birth _____

    Education _____

Adult life _____

    Married/to whom _____

    Children/their names _____

Achievements _____

People and events important to this person. _____

Interesting facts about this person _____

Date of death _____

If still alive, plans for the future _____

Attach pictures—photographs, photocopies, video clips, download from Internet.

Sources of my information _____

Interview Show

Directions:

1. Students research famous people, and/or athletic team members, patriotic groups, explorers, and so on, using the "Take Notes" sheets to record information.

2. One student pretends he or she is the person selected. Each person pretending to be a famous person will be a "guest" on an "interview show."

3. Set up a "set" for interviews. The set will be a table with a chair for the interviewer and a chair for the guest(s), with audience chairs.

4. The interviewer will prepare question cards, and use these to "interview" the guest. The guest will respond, based on the research already done.

Sample

Good afternoon. Today we are lucky to have _____ with us. As you know, _____ is famous for _____. Let's welcome _____.

1. When and where were you born?

2. Would you please tell us about your early years?

3. When did you know that you were "special"?

4. Did you receive any money, awards, or the like for your accomplishments?

5. What would you say was the *reason* you were able to become someone we all know?

6. Could you tell us about the things that make you famous?

7. We would like to have questions from the audience for our guest. Please raise your hand and ask your question for our guest.

Family Biography

Directions: Students interview someone in their families. The person should be a good deal older than the students. They can choose a grandparent or older aunt, or so on. Students should ask if they can video or audio record their conversations. They should be sure to ask the following questions and add more of their own.

When were you born? _____

Where did you grow up? (city, town, state) _____

When you were a kid, what did you want to be when you grew up? _____

What kinds of clothes did you wear to school? What did your hair look like? _____

What did you do for fun? _____

What do you remember most about being my age? _____

Did you have any pets? What were they? What were their names? _____

What was your best friend's name? _____

What was your favorite song or music group performer? _____

What was your favorite book? _____

Is there a historical event that has made a lasting impression on you? _____

If yes, what was the event and how did you feel when it happened? _____

Do you have a favorite picture of yourself that I can include in my report? _____

Students will decide how to present the information they have collected to the class. They could pretend to be a TV reporter, and could use their taped interviews if editing isn't necessary because of length or language.

You're Special

Directions: Students use a "special" biographical dictionary to locate information on their *special* people. They will do the following steps, using the form below.

1. Use names of the people you are studying in one of your subject areas or use a calendar of birthdays of famous people to choose a person to research.

2. Write three questions to learn about your special person.

3. Look up the person in a biographical dictionary.

   a. Write the information that answers your questions.

   b. Credit the dictionary using the bibliographical format.

4. Use another *print* research source to compare the information you have collected.

5. Use the *Internet* or a biographical *CD-ROM* program to compare the information.

After collecting the information, students can have a trivia-style quiz. Students could also be given the sources and have others try to locate the answers in the shortest length of time.

Person	Biographical Dictionary	Second Print Source	Electronic Resource
Question 1	Answer		
Question 2			
Question 3			

Biography Trading Cards

Directions:

1. Students research famous people, athletic team members, patriotic groups, explorers, and so on, using the "Take Notes" sheets to record information.

2. Students will then make the trading cards by drawing or pasting a picture of the subject on a piece of paper and adding information, such as accomplishments or anything the student would like to "remember" about his or her famous person. (Don't worry if different students choose the same person. The cards can be unique to each student.)

3. Students should make several copies of their subject so they will have "cards" to trade. They can use a copy machine to make their copies.

4. Students can display or trade cards.

5. Students can collect a "set," that is, of patriots, athletes, politicians, explorers, and so on.

6. Cards may be laminated for durability.

Name _____

Birth/Death dates _____

Set name _____

Accomplishments

_____

_____

_____

_____

Picture Collage

Directions: Use short autobiographies the students have written. Display baby pictures or early years pictures with a letter on each one, and display the autobiographies, with numbers on each one. Students will guess which pictures (letters) and autobiographies (numbers) go together and record their answers on a ballot.

Your name_____

Your guesses_____

Numbers and letters that go together

_____ and _____

Secret Identity

Directions: Number and display autobiographies and biographies. Students guess who the person is and write their guesses on a ballot.

Your name_____

Your guesses_____

Numbers and guesses

_____

_____

Cartoon Biography

Directions: Use autobiographies and biographies. Have students draw pictures in cartoon frames of events of a subject's life. Display cartoons for the class.

Biography of By	Early life	Important events		

NAME _____   DATE _____

Biographies

1. What is a biography?

2. What is an autobiography?

3. What is a collective biography?

4. What are the letters and other information on a biography spine label?

5. How are biographies shelved in a library?

6. What is the Dewey Classification number for collective biographies?

7. Is historical fiction good to use for biography research? Why or why not?

8. What is the advantage of using a biographical dictionary?

9. What is the disadvantage of using a biographical dictionary?

10. What are the advantages and disadvantages of using the Internet for biographical information?

Biography Jeopardy

Directions:

1. Students research famous people, and/or athletic team members, patriotic groups, explorers, and so on, using the "Trading Cards" (Activity 5.7) they have made for the answer cards.

2. Make and laminate a board using library card pockets. Write the categories on the chart, with "money" or points amounts as shown below.

3. Place answer cards in the pockets.

4. Divide students into teams. Teams choose a category and try to give a question for the answers.

5. Winning "questions" receive the "money" or points amount shown on the pocket. The team with the most money/points wins.

100	100	100	100	100
200	200	200	200	200
300	300	300	300	300
400	400	400	400	400
500	500	500	500	500
600	600	600	600	600
700	700	700	700	700
800	800	800	800	800
900	900	900	900	900
1000	1000	1000	1000	1000

LESSON 5-B

Bartlett's Familiar Quotations

To the Instructor

Bartlett's Familiar Quotations is used to find inspirational or patriotic quotes and words of wisdom that the population wants to remember. Students can locate titles of poems knowing a famous line, and they can connect words and phrases we use every day to the author of the extract.

Objectives

1. Students learn how to use the index key words in *Bartlett's Familiar Quotations* to locate authors and their works.

2. Students understand that alphabetization is word-for-word, not letter-by-letter.

3. Students learn how to use the numbers at the end of each entry to find the page of the quotation's author.

4. Students learn that the quotations are in chronological order.

5. Students learn how to credit quotations correctly in their written work.

Materials

Bartlett's Familiar Quotations, latest edition

Teaching and Preparation

1. Demonstrate how to find quotations.

2. Explain the correct way to give credit to the author of a famous quote.

3. Define ellipsis points or dots in quotations.

4. Review Internet references.

   http://education.yahoo.com/reference/bartlett

   http://www.bartleby.com/99/ (Bartlett's online)

   http://www.bartleby.com/66/ (Columbia World of Quotations)

   http://www.cyberquotations.com (Cyber quotations)

   http://www.aphids.com/quotes/ (Quotation archive)

   http://www.quoteland.com/ (Quoteland.com)

   http://www.bartleby.com/63/ (Simpson's Contemporary Quotations)

Activities

5.11 Copy Quotations ◨ ■

Display posters with famous quotes (no page) □ ◨ ■

Students write a statement they think will become a quotation to remember and create a poster with an illustration (no page) □ ◨ ■

Worksheet

5.2 Who Said…? □ ◨ ■

Connections to the Curriculum

Art—artist works

Language arts, science, and social studies—writing any paper with research entries from printed material

Music—excerpts used for presentations

Physical education—athletic records

Answer Key ....

WORKSHEET 5.2

1. Thomas Edison, *Life* (1932)
2. Pop artist Andy Warhol (1968)
3. Civil rights leader Martin Luther King Jr., speech at the March on Washington (Aug. 1963)
4. President Franklin D. Roosevelt, first inaugural address (Mar. 1933)
5. George Orwell, in the novel *1984* (1948)
6. George Lucas, screenplay for *Star Wars* (1977)
7. Attributed to baseball catcher Yogi Berra
8. Anthem of the civil rights movement
9. Neil Armstrong, the first person to set foot on the moon (July 1969)
10. Gertrude Stein, *Sacred Emily* (1913)

Copy Quotations

All books of quotations are written with the idea of collecting and appreciating words that should be remembered.

Quotation Subjects

Advertising slogans	Borrowed titles	Catchphrases
Closing lines	Epitaphs	Film lines
Film titles	Last words	Military sayings, slogans, and songs
Misquotations	Mottoes	Newspaper headlines and leaders
Official advice	Opening lines	Political slogans and songs
Prayers	Sayings and slogans	Songs, spirituals, and shanties
Telegrams	Toasts	

Quotable People

Presidents	Political leaders	Entertainers
Military leaders	Bible	Stories, poems, diaries, speeches
Royalty	Television	Anonymous (used when the author of a quote is unknown or cannot be identified)

Quotations can come from diaries, letters, speeches, and tombstones.

Directions: Students choose one of the categories from the list above and find a quotation from that category to illustrate, modernize, or update. They should research the person who said the quotation, and/or research the occasion of the quotation.

My quotation is "_____"

The source of my quotation is _____

I chose the quotation because _____

NAME _____   DATE _____

Who Said . . . ?

Directions: You are interested in finding out who said quotations that you hear in your daily life. Use *Bartlett's Familiar Quotations* to solve the mysteries. Write the person's name and origin of the quote on the lines below.

Who said . . . ?

1. "Genius is one percent inspiration and ninety-nine percent perspiration."   _____

2. "In the future everyone will be world-famous for fifteen minutes."   _____

3. "I have a dream . . . content of their character."   _____

4. "The only thing we have to fear is fear itself."   _____

5. "Big Brother is watching you."   _____

6. "May the force be with you."   _____

7. "It ain't over till it's over."   _____

8. "We shall overcome."   _____

9. "That's one small step for man, one giant leap for mankind."   _____

10. "Rose is a rose is a rose is a rose, is a rose."   _____

Using Reference Resources:
Current Information

LESSON 6-A

··

Introduction to Periodicals

To the Instructor ···

Students will use periodicals throughout their entire lives.

Objectives ···

1. Students understand how to use and read current information sources.

2. Students learn how to evaluate the current information in newspapers and magazines.

3. Students learn how to use the *Reader's Guide to Periodical Literature* to locate back magazine articles.

Materials ··

Transparency

    6.1 Periodicals ☐ ◧ ◼

Magazines
Newspapers
Reader's Guide to Periodical Literature

Teaching and Preparation . . . .

1. Skim various magazines and newspapers.

2. Discuss how to use the *Reader's Guide to Periodical Literature*.

3. Review Internet reference.

   http://www.cfr.org/press/publications/

Worksheet . . . .

6.1 Choose the Periodical ◨ ■

Connections to the Curriculum . . . .

Students will need current information in all curriculum areas.

Answer Key . . . .

WORKSHEET 6.1

1. E	5. D	8. A
2. G	6. B	9. F
3. J	7. I	10. C
4. H		

Periodicals

Periodicals are printed materials that are published at regular times or periods, usually daily, weekly, or monthly.

Breaking news   Events that happen after a paper has been printed. The publisher may choose to print a special edition to relay the information to the public.

Magazines   Publications printed weekly, monthly, bimonthly, or annually, catering to the public with special interests—sports, entertainment, home decorating, and so on.

Newspapers   Publications printed daily to give local, national, and/or international information. Newspapers can be published more than once a day.

Reader's Guide to Periodical Literature   Reference aid to locating articles published in magazines. The *Reader's Guide* lists magazine articles alphabetically by topics and by author. Large topics are subdivided by subheadings.

Special editions   Newspapers published because of breaking news.

Reading a Periodical for an Assignment

1. Set a purpose.

2. Use key words.

3. Look at the title, illustrations, headings, and first paragraph for clues about the topic of the article.

TRANSPARENCY 6.1

Choose the Periodical

Directions: Match the *topic* in the first column with the periodical, *magazine,* in the second column. Write the letter of the magazine on the line next to the topic.

Topic

1. Arts and entertainment _____

2. Health _____

3. Pets and animals _____

4. Sports _____

5. Science _____

6. Transportation _____

7. Computer games _____

8. Culture and society _____

9. Politics and government _____

10. Travel _____

Magazine

A. *Cherokee Observer*

B. *Traffic World*

C. *Roads to Adventure*

D. *Water World*

E. *TV Guide*

F. *City Journal*

G. *Nurse Week*

H. *Basketball Digest*

I. *Electronic Gaming Monthly*

J. *Cats & Kittens*

LESSON 6-B

Newspapers

To the Instructor

The library media center should have at least one daily newspaper for faculty and student reading. The newspaper should also be used for the vertical file clippings.

Objectives

1. Students learn how to locate different sections of the newspaper.

2. Students learn the terminology of newspapers.

3. Students learn how to apply newspapers to research.

4. Students learn the purposes of newspapers: they inform, entertain, interpret, persuade, and serve the community.

Materials

Transparency

6.2 Newspaper Glossary □ ◧ ■

A daily newspaper (lesson could be done during Newspapers in Education Week to provide a newspaper for each student)

Teaching and Preparation ....

1. Demonstrate the various sections of a newspaper.

2. Use newspaper terms to teach the learning activities.

3. Locate articles using the newspaper index.

4. Review Internet references.

   http://dir.yahoo.com/News_and_Media/Newspapers/ (Yahoo directory of newspapers)

   http://www.newslink.org (Newslink)

   http://library.uncg.edu/news/ (news and newspapers)

   http://www.yahooligans.yahoo.com/reference/encyclopedia/entry?id=33841

   http://www.yahooligans.yahoo.com/arts_and_entertainment/news/newspapers

   http://www.ipl.org/div/news

Activities ....

6.1 The Five W's and How ☐ ◪ ■

6.2 Newspaper Photos ◪ ■

6.3 Travel with the Newspaper ☐ ◪ ■

6.4 Compare Newspapers ◪ ■

Worksheets ....

6.2 Newspaper Index ☐ ◪

6.3 Photojournalist ☐ ◪ ■

6.4 Comics ☐ ◪

6.5 Mock Newspaper ☐ ◪

6.6 Figures of Speech ■

Games ....

6.1 Got a Minute? ☐ ◪ ■

6.2 Newspaper Scavenger Hunt I ☐ ◪ ■

6.3 Newspaper Scavenger Hunt II ☐ ◪ ■

Connections to the Curriculum ....

Students should use the newspaper for all subject areas and recreational reading (comics, features, entertainment, and so on).

Math—learn about purchasing a car, or finding a house or apartment for a certain price

Reading and social studies—learn about current events and use a map to locate where the stories come from

Science—look for advances in science, such as cures for diseases, space travel, and so on

Answer Key ....

WORKSHEET 6.2

1. Everyday section
2. Front page
3. Sports section
4. Classified advertising section
5. Comics page
6. Classified advertising section
7. Features or entertainment section
8. Front page
9. Retail advertising (throughout newspaper)
10. Editorial page
11. Community/metropolitan section
12. National/international section

Newspaper Glossary

5W1H   Questions that are answered by news stories: who, what, why, where, when, and how.

Advertising   Lists or displays of things that are for sale.

Angle   The point of view of the person writing the article.

Banner headline   First line after the name of the paper printed with the largest words, often going across the entire front page.

Beat   A reporter's regular routine, or area of reportage.

Byline   The identification of the writer of the article.

Cartoon   A drawing caricaturing or symbolizing, often satirically, some event or person of topical interest.

Circulation   The average number of paid copies a newspaper distributes.

Classified ads   Advertisements compactly arranged according to subject. Can include births and deaths announcements.

Column inch   Space measurement to determine the length of a story: vertical inch, one column wide.

Columns   Vertical, easy-reading sections to help pick out news items.

Comic strips   Series or cartoons usually telling a humorous story.

Copy   All written materials prepared for publications, including articles, cutlines, and written materials for ads.

Cutline   Caption that appears under a photo or illustration to explain it.

Dateline   Line at the beginning of a news story that gives the location of the story's origin. It is the date and place of writing the article.

Edition   Different versions of the newspaper for late-breaking news and statistics. Stars represent the edition number. Dots represent the number of page lifts during the press run.

Editorial   A statement of opinion.

Editorial cartoon   Graphic that expresses opinions and interprets news.

Feature   Story dealing with something other than late-breaking news.

Flag   Nameplate of the newspaper on the front page.

Freelancer   A reporter who is not under contract for regular work but whose writing or services are sold to individual papers.

Graphic   Computer design or illustration generated by the newspaper.

Headline   A line of words usually in larger type at the top of a newspaper article giving a short statement of its contents; the title of a newspaper story. The headline is designed to grab the reader's attention.

Index   List, often boxed, of what is to be found inside the newspaper and where it is located.

Jump   Continuation of a story from one page to another.

Jump line   Copy that tells readers on what page a story is continued.

Layout (dummy)   Plan or makeup of a newspaper indicating where ads, stories, headlines, and so on are to be placed.

Lead   Opening line of a news story. It usually is a summary of the most important information.

Masthead   Name of the newspaper.

Morgue   The collection of back numbers, photographs, and clippings kept in the office.

News   Articles that give information that people need to know immediately.

Online services   Information provided electronically on the Internet.

Paste up   Organizing the articles of a newspaper on a page for fit and importance.

Photo   Graphic using a camera.

Photojournalist   A person who uses a camera rather than words to tell the story.

Prepress   Department where the newspaper is prepared for production. Photos are scanned into computers, news and ads are printed on photographic paper, and page negatives are made.

Press   Machine that prints a newspaper.

Publisher   A person responsible for the total operation of a newspaper.

Pull quote   A graphic device in which a quote is taken from a news story and displayed in a box within the story.

Rail   Column down the left side of the front page or first page of a section highlighting stories inside.

Reporter   A person who gathers information and writes reports for publication.

Sidebar   Additional information for quick reference in a box near a longer story.

Skybox   Block of information placed above the flag, or name, of the newspaper.

Summary deck   Type located below the headline, giving extra details about a story.

Syndicate   A news service that sells columns, comics, and specialty features.

Teaser   Type that tells the readers what other interesting stories appear in that day's edition.

Top story   The story that appears at the top right of the front page. It has the most important news of the day. It has the larger headline and more space.

Wire service   News-gathering agency that distributes news and photos to subscribing papers. It is a national or international news service that distributes electronically to newspapers around the country or the world.

The Five W's and How

Directions: The main purpose of news stories is to inform. New stories are written in the inverted pyramid style, giving the reader the most important information in the lead. The lead is the first paragraph of a news story answering the questions who, what, when, where, why, and how.

Students should read and choose two news stories. They may also use fairy tales or other stories they like. They will then describe the "W's" they found, using a copy of the chart below.

Who	What	When	Why	Where	How

Newspaper Photos

Directions: News photos often tell a story by themselves. Photos can stand alone; those that do are referred to as "wild photos." Students will use local newspapers for collages and other projects.

Individual

Students look through their copy of the newspaper to find and clip eight to ten news photos that they think are especially interesting, then do the following:

1. Assemble the pictures and write interesting real-story information for each one.

2. Use the pictures and write make-believe captions or cutlines to make a new and interesting story.

Group

In a small group, create a whole new story about recent news events in your school. Have group members use photos to help illustrate the story. The photos may be shot at your school or may be unrelated pictures cut from your local newspaper and made to seem like they were taken at your school. Encourage the students to be creative, humorous, and/or outrageous.

Variation

Choose a photo and have students write declarative, interrogative, exclamatory, and imperative sentences for that same picture.

Travel with the Newspaper

Directions: Use a travel section of your newspaper. Students will do the following:

1. Clip pictures of a country and read articles about this particular place.

2. Use an atlas and find a map of the city with the surrounding areas.

3. Make a map of the city with the places (historical, entertaining) that you would want to visit.

4. Use a large map and show the travel route from your home city to the country or city.

5. Make postcards that you would send to your friends.

   A. Draw a picture of a place on one side.

   B. On the opposite side, write a "wish you were here" description of your destination.

Compare Newspapers

Directions: Students use the vertical files to compare newspapers, either individually or in groups. They will do the following:

1. Compare newspapers from the Civil War period, World War I, and World War II, or from three other different time periods.

2. Make a chart to show how headlines, advertisements, and stories are arranged by different editors and time periods. The chart can resemble the one shown below.

Time periods compared: _____

Types of papers (local, national): _____

Evaluation with regard to first amendment of the Constitution:

_____

Name	Headlines	Advertisements	Stories

NAME _____ DATE _____

Newspaper Index

Directions: The best place to find current information for entertainment and information about your hometown is the newspaper. Use the index of your hometown newspaper to answer the following questions. Write the page on which you would find the information.

Where would you find information about . . .

1. A crossword puzzle or game?

2. The weather forecast?

3. The final scores and stories about a sports team?

4. A used automobile for sale?

5. Cartoon characters?

6. A new job opportunity?

7. A movie to take your little brother to?

8. The most important news of the day?

9. Advertisements for something new to wear?

10. A letter of opinion about a current event?

11. A story about your city?

12. A story about a foreign city?

NAME   DATE

Photojournalist

Do you think that words and pictures always go together? Look for a photograph that interests you. Read the article that accompanies the photo. Cut out the photo and paste it in the box below. Under the photo make a caption for the photo and then write a short article about the photo.

NAME _____ DATE _____

Comics

Directions: Do you like the comics page of the newspaper? Look through the comic strips. Find a character you like. Cut and paste one frame from the strip here. Change the words in the bubble to say something new. Make the character say something about a special event, the environment, or something in your school. Make a list of other comic strips that you like and in the second column why you like them. (Don't say because they are funny.)

Comic Strips I Like	The Reason I Like Them

NAME _____ DATE _____

Mock Newspaper

Directions: There is not enough space to print stories about everything that happens every day. Someone has to decide what to print. That person is the editor of the newspaper.

1. Make a list of five things that have happened recently in your school or community.

   _____   _____

   _____   _____

   _____

2. Decide what to put on the front page of your newspaper. You only have room for four of your story suggestions.

3. Design your front page. Use headlines and draw pictures to go with each story.

My Newspaper

NAME _____ DATE _____

Figures of Speech

Directions: Skim the newspaper to see which parts of the newspaper might be most likely to contain figures of speech. Find as many examples as possible.

Irony (meaning the opposite of what is expressed)	
Metaphor (one thing is said to represent another very different object)	
Satire (use of sarcasm to poke fun at someone)	
Simile (comparing two unlike objects using "like" or "as")	
Hyperbole (an exaggeration or extravagant statement)	

Got a Minute?

Directions:

A. The object of the game is for students to find the most items in the newspaper as fast as they can. The librarian can use the list below or develop his or her own list according to age and time allotment.

B. Students will need a copy of a newspaper, a sheet of paper, and a pen or pencil.

C. Students find and write down the following. The winner is the one who has the most correct answers first.

1. The scoreboard for a sports team

2. A comic strip with an animal in it

3. The weather in your city

4. The time of a (television) show

5. A kids' page of interest

6. An advertisement for a movie

7. Five words beginning with the letter "B" on the first page

8. A used car for sale

9. A game or puzzle

10. A number larger than a million

Newspaper Scavenger Hunt I

Directions: Teams write down the page numbers where each scavenger item is found. The first team to find all the items is the winner.

1. A date other than today

2. The high temperature in a major city

3. A face with glasses

4. An international dateline

5. A city within one hundred miles of your hometown

6. A vehicle other than a car

7. A movie that starts between 7:00 and 9:00 P.M.

8. A compound word

9. The name of a TV show that ends at 9:00 P.M.

10. A politician

11. An example of good news

12. Something hot

13. Something that makes you smile

Newspaper Scavenger Hunt II

Directions: Teams write down the page numbers on which each scavenger item is found. The first team to find all the items is the winner.

1. A picture of someone wearing a hat

2. A map

3. A picture of an animal

4. A television listing

5. The name of your city

6. A picture of a sport

7. An action word

8. The name of a television star

9. A cartoon

10. A story about another country

11. A letter from a reader

12. A movie review or ad

LESSON 6-C

Magazines

To the Instructor

A wide and varied collection of magazines, plus the *Reader's Guide to Periodical Literature* and the *Children's Magazine Guide,* are excellent research tools.

Objectives

1. Students learn to use current issues of magazines for recreational reading.

2. Students familiarize themselves with the organization of articles in magazines.

3. Students learn how to apply current and back issues of magazines as research tools.

4. Students learn how to use the *Reader's Guide to Periodical Literature* and/or the *Children's Magazine Guide* to locate articles in issues of magazines.

Materials

Transparency

6.3 Magazine Glossary □ ◧ ■

Current and back issues of magazines
Reader's Guide to Periodical Literature

Children's Magazine Guide
Online computer

Teaching and Preparation ....

1. Use the table of contents or index of a magazine to find articles.

2. Discuss magazine production.

3. Demonstrate the *Reader's Guide* and *Children's Magazine Guide* for finding magazine articles.

4. Review Internet references.

   http://www.yahooligans.com/school_bell/language_arts/Magazines

   http://www.MagPortal.com

   http://www.metagrid.com

   http://www.publist.com

Activity ....

6.5 Magazine Cover ☐ ◪

Worksheets ....

6.7 Magazine Selection ◪ ■

6.8 Magazines ☐ ◪

6.9 Magazine Research ☐ ◪ ■

Connections to the Curriculum ....

Magazines can be used in every area of the curriculum.

Answer Key ....

WORKSHEETS 6.7 AND 6.9

Answers will vary.

WORKSHEET 6.8

1. A. Title of the magazine

   B. Pictures of people and things in the magazine

   C. Cost of the magazine

   D. Titles of articles in the magazine

   E. Date the magazine was published

2. No. Each magazine editor chooses his or her own format.

3. The editor chooses the articles, cover, and arrangement and placement of material within the magazine.

4. A subscription means you have paid to receive the magazine on a regular basis, usually for a year or longer.

5. Readers are able to give their opinions about anything appearing in the magazine.

6. Advertisements give businesses a way to communicate with potential customers for their product. They also help the publisher with the cost of producing the magazine.

7. Magazines can be published weekly, bimonthly, monthly, or semiannually.

Magazine Glossary

Advertisements   Print ads placed in a magazine for products usually associated with the subject of the magazine, to be sold to readers.

Children's Magazine Guide   A special publication to find information located in children's magazines, with the following categories: subject heading; article title; author; and magazine name, date, and pages.

Editor   Person who decides what articles are in a magazine and the order in which they are placed.

Issue   The volume of the magazine that is published, either weekly, biweekly, or monthly.

Letters to the editor   Reader's comments about articles published in a special section as another view of an article.

Magazine index guide   A publication that lists magazines and stories you will find within them. The information is listed alphabetically by subject.

Number   Each copy of a magazine is numbered beginning with 1 for the first copy of the year, 2 for the second, and so on.

Reader's Guide to Periodical Literature   A book that is an index of magazine articles. Magazine articles appear alphabetically by subject and author, in the following categories: subject heading; article title; author; and magazine name, volume, date, and pages.

Subscription   A prepaid arrangement to have a magazine delivered to one's home for a length of time. Usually the cost is reduced because a person has made a commitment to purchase the magazine for at least a year.

Table of contents   Page that lists the title of a story, the author, and the page number on which it starts. Stories are usually listed in the order in which they will appear. The table of contents also often shows the publisher name and mailing address, and the price of the magazine.

Volume   All copies of a magazine published during one year. Every issue of a magazine in a year has the same volume number.

Magazine Cover

Directions: Students design a cover for a monthly magazine, including titles, pictures, volume, price, and teasers that will make people want to read the articles. Students can display or compare their covers when finished.

NAME _____   DATE _____

Magazine Selection

Directions: You want to give your brother a present for his birthday. Find a magazine to give him. Look at the magazines in your library media center and find one that will be perfect for him. Fill in the information below.

Magazine name:

Volume:

Number:

Date:

1. How often is the magazine published?

2. What is the cost of a single copy?

3. What is the cost for a yearly subscription?

4. Would you pay the same price if you lived in Canada?

5. What is the copyright information of the magazine?

6. What is the address of the magazine publisher?

7. Does the magazine have a table of contents?

8. Are the contents of the magazine listed by departments?

9. If so, what are the departments listed?

NAME _____ DATE _____

Magazines

1. Name the information found on the cover of a magazine.

   A.

   B.

   C.

   D.

   E.

2. Are all magazine table of contents pages arranged the same way? Why or why not?

3. What does the editor of a magazine do?

4. What is a subscription?

5. What is the purpose of a letters to the editor section?

6. Why do magazines have advertisements?

7. How often are magazines published?

NAME _____   DATE _____

Magazine Research

Directions: Choose a magazine and answer the following questions. Be prepared to discuss with other students why this magazine would be useful in a research project.

1. Write the title of the magazine.

2. Write the month and year of publication of the magazine.

3. Study the magazine and answer the following questions:

   A. Who would be interested in this magazine?

   B. How often is the magazine published?

   C. How much does the magazine cost?

   D. Does the magazine have fiction and/or nonfiction stories?

   E. Does the magazine have illustrations?

   F. Does the magazine have games or puzzles?

   G. Could you use this magazine to do a research paper? If yes, name the subjects or key words.

   H. Is this magazine for recreational reading?

LESSON 6-D

Reader's Guide to Periodical Literature

To the Instructor

The *Reader's Guide to Periodical Literature* is used in locating information in magazines. An extensive magazine and archive collection is essential.

Objectives

1. Students learn how to use the *Reader's Guide* to locate articles that have appeared in well-known magazines.

2. Students learn how to use the *Reader's Guide* to find up-to-date information and a volume of the same magazine on the same subject from the past.

Materials

Transparency

6.4 *Reader's Guide to Periodical Literature* □ ◧ ■

Copy of the *Reader's Guide to Periodical Literature*
Online computer

Teaching and Preparation ....

1. Demonstrate how to use the index of the *Reader's Guide.*

2. Access the online *Reader's Guide* and locate the same information.

3. Discuss a sample subject entry of article title, magazine citation, volume number, paging, date of magazine, illustrations, and author.

4. Use a sample name entry of the author and subject.

5. Locate the individual magazines in your library media center.

6. Review Internet references.

   http://www.lib.duke.edu/reference/prinindex/readguid.htm

   http://www.findarticles.com/ (Find articles.com)

Worksheet ....

6.10 *Reader's Guide* ❑◼ ◼

Connections to the Curriculum ....

The social studies teacher should use the *Reader's Guide* to develop techniques for searching for magazines and recent news items. Newspapers should also be used for this project, and a comparison of the views of various reporters should be discussed.

Answer Key ....

WORKSHEET 6.10

1. A. B. Tierney
   B. Toys for Young and Old
   C. *Fun and Games*
   D. July 8, 1999
   E. 26–28
   F. 12
2. Dolls
3. Answers will vary, but sentence should mention dolls and toys.
4. Toys

Reader's Guide to Periodical Literature

Use the *Reader's Guide* to …

1. Find the editions of magazines you need (month/year).

2. Look up the subject alphabetically.

3. Look up an author's last name.

4. Check cross-references (guides toward more information).

5. Write down facts about articles you want to read.

6. Locate the magazines

Author entry   Last name comma first name

Cross-references   *See*

Subject entry   All capital letters

Title of entry   Words of title in quotation marks

Name, author, title, volume, and number of magazine

Page numbers, month, and year

Space Vehicles
See also   Space Stations
                  Space Stations
                  Space Tugs
21st-century spacecraft [Pluto Fast Fly-by and the Kuiper Express]
F. J. Dyson. Il Scientific American
V273 p114–116A S '95

TRANSPARENCY 6.4

Reader's Guide

DOLLS
Toys for Young and Old. B. Tierney. *Fun and Games* 12:26–28
Jul 8 '99

Directions: Use the entry above from the *Reader's Guide* to answer the following questions.

1. Locate the author, article title, magazine title, date of publication, page numbers, and volume number. Write them on the following lines.

    A. Author _____

    B. Article title _____

    C. Magazine title _____

    D. Date of publication _____

    E. Page numbers _____

    F. Volume number _____

2. Under what subject word was the article found?

3. Write a sentence describing what you think this article is about.

4. Under what other subjects might you find more information?

LESSON 6-E

Vertical Files

To the Instructor

Middle schools should have a vertical file collection. Students or adult volunteers are needed to update the collections and keep them current. Elementary schools also should have an archive of historical information from newspapers and magazines, large maps, and posters.

Objectives

1. Students become skilled at locating newspapers, pictures, maps, and the like in the vertical file.

2. Students recognize the value of saving current historical information found in newspapers and magazines.

3. Students learn how to use oversized pictures, pamphlets, or posters from the vertical file to create displays and bulletin boards for holidays or special events.

Materials

Vertical file
Newspapers
Magazines
Pictures

Teaching and Preparation

1. Demonstrate vertical file information.

2. Use current newspaper articles to explain how information is added to the vertical file.

3. Review Internet references.

   http://www.pickerington.lib.oh.us/policy.html

   http://www.lasalle-academy.org/libr/verticalfiles.html

Activities

6.6 Compare Various Sources ◨ ■

6.7 Story Board ☐ ◨ ■

6.8 Create Visual Aids ☐ ◨ ■

Connections to the Curriculum

The social studies curriculum should include current information. Students in seventh and eighth grades should be required to read the newspaper. They should learn how to look for articles that will be of historical interest or needed at a later time to collaborate a current events assignment. The school newspaper should contribute its issues to the vertical file.

Compare Various Sources

Directions: Students compare newspapers and other available materials from the Civil War period, World War I, World War II, or other time periods you are studying, using the library files. They can also compare one past time period to today.

Using the blank chart below, students will follow these instructions:

1. Write the topics you are researching in the first column. Sample topics to compare are fashion, headlines, sports, advertisements, cartoons, or world leaders.

2. Compare your birth date—for example, May 20—to different time periods: May 20, 1900; May 20, 2000; and so on.

3. In the columns, write the years you are using for your research time period. Include the name of your research source.

Example: World War I, The 1920s, Today's date.

Topic	Time Period One	Time Period Two

Story Board

Directions: Students look through the vertical files for interesting picture ideas that will start their own story, and photocopy the picture or cartoon. Remind them to give credit to their source.

Students will place the picture in frame one of their board, then draw the other frames to make their story. Stories can be shared or compared with other students when finished.

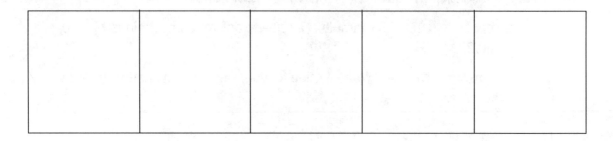

Create Visual Aids

Directions: Students will do the following:

1. Look through the library's collection of pictures, maps, illustrations, and so on.

2. Photocopy or make a transparency of pictures from the newspaper or magazine. Be sure to credit the source.

3. Enlarge or reduce the pictures to fit the notebook, bulletin board space, or other medium chosen to present the visual aid.

4. Color the transparency, or mount the picture appropriately.

5. Include a caption for your aid.

6. Display or share with other students.

LESSON 6-F

Outside the Library Media Center

To the Instructor ....

There are many resources outside the library media center. These resources can make reports interesting and unique.

Objectives ....

1. Students become aware of reference resources that are outside the library media center.

2. Students learn how to use reference resources that are outside the library media center.

Materials ....

Lists of resources outside the library media center

Teaching and Preparation . . . .

1. Display a list of resources outside the library media center.

2. Brainstorm with the students for unique resources.

3. Show students how to locate information on a subject using an outside source and report back to the class.

Activity . . . .

6.9 Outside Resources Report ☐ ◫ ■

Connections to the Curriculum . . . .

Students should be able to use the community around them to obtain information for reports and special interests. All areas of the curriculum should use these resources.

Outside Resources Report

Potential Outside Resources

1. Archives of various institutions (schools, churches, etc.)
2. Brochures
3. Businesses
4. Chamber of Commerce
5. Experiments
6. Field guides
7. Genealogy study
8. Government agencies (federal, state, city)
9. Historical sites
10. Historical societies
11. Hospitals
12. Internet (e-mail)
13. Museums
14. Observations
15. Personal letters
16. Police station
17. Post office
18. Radio or television stations
19. Surveys
20. Telephone books
21. Travel agency
22. Tourist bureaus
23. Zoo

Directions:

Students contact one or two of the outside resources listed above and report to the class.

Students should name the "source" and tell what kind of information is available from it.

Students should ask the "source" to mail information to your school in the librarian's name.

UNIT
SEVEN

Dewey Decimal Classification System

LESSON 7-A

....

Dewey Decimal Classification System

To the Instructor ....

The Dewey Decimal Classification System is used for organizing all nonfiction materials in school and public libraries.

Objectives ....

1. Students learn about Melvil Dewey.

2. Students gain knowledge of the ten major classification areas of the Dewey Decimal System.

3. Students learn how to use the Dewey Decimal System sheet to locate nonfiction resources.

Materials ....

Transparency

7.1 Dewey Decimal Classification Numbers ☐ ◨ ■

Dewey Decimal Classification System sheets
Biography of Melvil Dewey
Online computer

Teaching and Preparation ....

1. Introduce Melvil Dewey and his contributions to library science. Use overhead projector to share Dewey's biography or use Internet biography site for demonstration: http://www.encyclopedia.com/articlesnew/03618.html.

2. Review Internet references.

   http://www.oclc.org/dewey/

   http://www.mtsu/~vvesper/dewey.html

   http://www.bcpl.gov.bc.ca/VRD/helpdesk/dewey.php

   http://www.ipl.org/div/books

Activities ....

7.1 Dewey and the Alien □ ◻■

7.2 Searching for Dewey □ ◻■

On small cards, write the numbers 100, 200, 300, and so on and attach the cards to boxes or folders. Cut pictures out of magazines of items that fit the ten major areas of the Dewey Decimal System and have students place the pictures in the correct box or folder. (no page) □ ◻■ ■

Students look through magazines to find pictures for a specific category and place the picture in the correct folder. Check for understanding and accuracy. (no page) □ ◻■ ■

Worksheets ....

7.1 Dewey Pictures □ ◻■

7.2 Practicing Dewey □ ◻■ ■

Game ....

7.1 Dewey Jeopardy □ ◻■ ■

Connections to the Curriculum ....

Students will be able to locate materials on the shelves without going to the card or electronic catalogs.

Answer Key ....

ACTIVITY 7.1

A. To learn about the Dewey Classification System
B. A UFO and an Alien
C. Who are you? (100) Where did you come from? (200)
D. To your leader (300)
E. How to communicate (400)
F. Life on planet Earth (500)
G. Change it (600)
H. Basketball (700)
 I. Write poems, stories, and plays (800)
J. Made a scrapbook (900)
K. Organize his books (000–999)

ACTIVITY 7.2

A. 1851
B. 1883–1889
C. The first library training school
D. The vertical office file
E. The American Library Association
F. 1931

WORKSHEET 7.1

 900
 000
 700
 600
 200

 000
 300/400
 100/400
 500

 800
 300
 700
 200

WORKSHEET 7.2

A.	rocks 500	P.	Civil War 900
B.	Bibles 200	Q.	geography 900
C.	tennis 700	R.	travel 900
D.	sculpture 700	S.	plays 800
E.	logic 100	t.	Big Foot 100
F.	birds 500	u.	stars 500
G.	fairy tales 300	V.	music 700
H.	toads 500	W.	poetry 800
I.	Spanish language 400	X.	Germany 900
J.	computers 600	Y.	hockey 700
K.	pet care 600	Z.	laws 300
L.	space travel 600	aa.	atlas 000 and 900
M.	fish 500	bb.	planets 500
N.	paintings 700	cc.	cooking 700
O.	encyclopedias 000	dd.	baseball 700

Dewey Decimal Classification Numbers

Every nonfiction book in the library media center is assigned a decimal number corresponding to its subject matter. This classification system was developed by Melvil Dewey in 1876.

000–099	General Books	Reference, books about books, encyclopedias
100–199	Philosophy	All about me (thinking and feeling)
200–299	Religion	All about God
300–399	Social Sciences	Getting along, folklore, holidays
400–499	Language	Communicating
500–599	Pure Sciences	Nature, the world, the universe
600–699	Technology	Using science
700–799	The Arts	Enjoying myself, music, art, recreation
800–899	Literature	Poetry, novels
900–999	Geography and History	Land, people, and events of the world

	400 Language	800 Literature	914 Geography	940 History
		810-American		
2-English	420-English	820-English	914.2-England	942-England
3-German	430-German	830-German	914.3-Germany	943-Germany
4-France	440-French	840-French	914.4-France	944-France
5-Italy	450-Italian	850-Italian	914.5-Italy	945-Italy
6-Spain	460-Spanish	860-Spanish	914.6-Spain	946-Spain
7-Latin	470-Latin	870-Latin		
8-Greek	480-Greek	880-Greek	914.8-Greece	948-Greece
9-Other	490-Other	890-Other*	914-9-Other	949-Other
				950-Asia
				960-Africa
				970-North America
				980-South America
				990-Other Parts of the World

* Chinese, Japanese, etc.

Dewey and the Alien

Directions: Students use the online computer to find information about Dewey and the Alien (http://tqjunior.thinkquest.org/5002/Alien/alien.htm), a very cute way to learn about the Dewey Decimal System that was developed by students. Have students answer the following questions and assign a Dewey Decimal classification number to answers C through K.

A. Why did the students write this story?

B. What did Dewey see in Central Park?

C. What two questions did Dewey and the Alien ask each other?

D. Where did the Alien want to be taken?

E. What did Dewey and the Alien have to learn?

F. What did Dewey have to explain?

G. What did humans do to nature?

H. What game did Dewey and the Alien play?

I. What do people do in their spare time?

J. What did Dewey and the Alien do when they visited the library?

K. What was the Alien going to do when he got back home?

Searching for Dewey

Directions: Show students how to use your online computer to find information about Melvil Dewey. Go to http://www.encyclopedia.com/html/d/dewey-m1e.asp, part of the Columbia Electronic Encyclopedia, 6th edition. Have students discover the following information.

A. When was Melvil Dewey born?

B. When was he the librarian at Columbia College?

C. What did he begin at Columbia College?

D. What is Dewey credited with inventing?

E. What organization did he begin?

F. When did he die?

NAME_____ DATE_____

Dewey Pictures

Directions: Use the information to identify what Dewey Decimal classes the pictures represent. Write the numbers below the pictures.

Ten Dewey Classification Divisions

000–099	General books	Reference, books about books, encyclopedias
100–199	Philosophy	All about me (thinking and feeling)
200–299	Religion	All about God
300–399	Social sciences	Getting along, folklore, holidays
400–499	Language	Communicating
500–599	Pure sciences	Nature, the world, the universe
600–699	Technology	Using science
700–799	The arts	Enjoying myself, music, art, recreation
800–899	Literature	Poetry, novels
900–999	Geography and history	The land, people, and events of the world

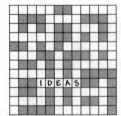

Practicing Dewey

Directions: Practice determining which Dewey number would include these key words. Write the number on the line following the key word.

Example: cats __500__

A. rocks _____

B. Bibles _____

C. tennis _____

D. sculpture _____

E. logic _____

F. birds _____

G. fairy tales _____

H. toads _____

I. Spanish language _____

J. computers _____

K. pet care _____

L. space travel _____

M. fish _____

N. paintings _____

O. encyclopedias _____

P. Civil War _____

Q. geography _____

R. travel _____

S. plays _____

T. Big Foot _____

U. stars _____

V. music _____

W. poetry _____

X. Germany _____

Y. hockey _____

Z. laws _____

aa. atlas _____

bb. planets _____

cc. cooking _____

dd. baseball _____

Dewey Jeopardy

Directions: This game is played after the students have learned the ten major Dewey classifications, and will help them reinforce their knowledge of those classifications.

A. Make a pocket chart with the ten major Dewey classes at the top. Include ten slots under each class to house cards.

B. Prepare many 3 x 5 inch cards with subjects or titles that will fit the Dewey classes (100 to 1000) and place in a deck face down.

C. Divide the students into teams of two to four players.

D. Students or the librarian will choose ten cards from the deck.

E. Start the timer.

F. Students try to place the cards in the correct slots.

G. The winner is the team with the most correct answers in the least amount of time.

UNIT
EIGHT

Fiction

LESSON 8-A

Books from Cover to Cover

To the Instructor ....

Students should be familiar with book terminology, and understand that the library has two kinds of books: fiction and nonfiction.

Objectives ....

1. Students learn terminology.

2. Students learn how to construct covers, jackets, and illustrations for publishing a book.

3. Students learn how to develop their own book ideas.

Materials ....

Transparencies

8.1 Book Glossary ☐ ◧ ■

8.2 Fiction ☐ ◧ ■

8.3 Nonfiction ☐ ◧ ■

8.4 Building a Story ☐ ◧ ■

Books or pages marked with the names of the parts.

Teaching and Preparation . . . .

1. Exhibit the different parts of a book.

2. Locate the book parts in other books.

3. Review Internet references.

   http://gutenberg.hwg.org/markup1a.html

   http://www.yahooligans.com/School_Bell/Language_Arts/Books/Reading_Lists/

Activities . . . .

8.1 Dust Jacket □ ◘

8.2 Spine Labels □ ◘

Worksheets . . . .

8.1 Cause and Effect ◘ ■

8.2 Characters □ ◘

Connections to the Curriculum . . . .

All areas of the curriculum will be affected by the student's ability to locate the different parts of a book.

Answer Key . . . .

WORKSHEET 8.1

Answers will vary.

WORKSHEET 8.2

Fairy Tales	Science Fiction	Biography
1. Dragon	Alien, Inventor	President, Princess
2. Elf	Robot, Astronaut	Explorer
3. Giant	Big Foot	Inventor
4. Witch	Vampire	Athlete
5. Princess	Ghost	Astronaut

Book Glossary

Acknowledgments Credit given by the author to persons who motivated or helped to give ideas for writing the book.

Action The dramatic events that move a story along.

Adventure Type of fast-paced book in which there is often a brave hero or heroine who is in danger.

Afterword Section at the end of a book used to bring the story to a conclusion.

Anthology A collection of any kind of literature.

Appendix Additional information added at the end of a book.

Author The person who wrote the book.

Awards The Newbery for best children's book, or the Caldecott for best illustrations, or any other recognitions for good literature.

Back cover The outside cover of a book or dust jacket with information about the book such as the teaser, summary, reviews, and awards.

Back flap The folded part of a dust jacket. It has information about the author and illustrator of the book.

Beginning The start of a book where the characters are introduced and the plot of the story is revealed.

Bibliography A list of other books to supplement the material in the book.

Blurb Information about a book written on the back of the dust jacket to make potential readers want to purchase or borrow it. In newspapers or magazines, comments about the book by an editor or other persons, sometimes called the review.

Body Text, maps, and illustrations within the book. May be chapters or some other divisions of a book.

Case Another name for the covers of a hardbound book.

Chapter A division of a book to show time changes, scene changes, subject changes, action changes, or thought changes.

Characters   People, or animals with human characteristics, around whom the story's action revolves.

Climax   The most exciting part of a book, usually when the plot is brought to a head or resolved.

Colophon   An embellishment to give brief descriptions of the facts of production.

Conclusion   At the end of a book, used to bring it to a close.

Copyright   The exclusive rights of an author and publisher to protect their ideas from plagiarists.

Copyright page   The page in the book that names the publisher and cataloging information registration. The dedication page can also have the copyright information.

Copyright symbol   The c in a circle after or before a publisher's name. It is used to show the publisher has permission to use the material from the author.

Cover   The outside of a book. It can be a hardbound book or a paperback.

Dedication page   A page with a note to people who were helpful to the author and whom he or she wishes to acknowledge.

Description   Detail used to create a visual image for the reader.

Dialogue   Conversations between characters in the story.

Diaries   Daily personal writings, often over years, used in writing a book.

Drama   Plotting in stories written to keep the reader on edge and wondering what will happen next. *See also* Play.

Dust jacket   A paper cover to protect the book. The front inside flap usually talks about the book. The back inside flap usually talks about the author. Information about the contents of the book can be seen on the back of the jacket.

End   The part of the story from the climax to the conclusion of the book. It is a wrap-up of the story.

Endpapers   The blank pages added between the cover and the rest of the written and illustrated pages of the text.

Epigraph   A pertinent quotation or statement.

Epilogue   A closing section added to a novel providing further information. An epilogue may be as long as a chapter and keep the formatting of a chapter.

 **TRANSPARENCY 8.1 cont.**

Fable   A short fiction story, usually about animals, created to teach a lesson or moral.

Fantasy   A work of fiction that is highly imaginative. It contains beings or events that could not exist.

Folktale   A work of fiction that contains legendary elements and is handed down orally among the common people. It can be a belief or story passed on traditionally and considered to be false or based on tradition.

Footnotes   Information supplementary to the text, often at the bottom of a page.

Foreword   An introduction by someone other than the author, often a famous person.

Front flap   The folded part of a dust jacket with information about the contents of the book.

Frontispiece   The picture opposite the title page.

Genre   The kind, type, or category of a story.

Glossary   A dictionary at the back of the book with the definitions of difficult words from the text in the book.

Gutter   The depression made when the pages of a book meet. Book pages are glued or sewn together.

Half title   The title page on two separate pages containing half of the information on each page. There may also be additional information such as an illustration. The half-title page usually only relates the title of the book.

Hardbound book   A book that has cardboard sheets to strengthen the pages of its construction.

Historical fiction   A story using a fact of history as the plot. The characters and events did not really exist but use the background for their story development.

Horror   A fictional story designed to keep readers on edge. There is often an evil character who must be overcome.

Illustrations   Pictures of the story. They may be paintings, photos, etc.

Illustrator   The person who drew the pictures or used some other form to have something other than words on the pages.

Index   An alphabetical list of subjects in the book showing the pages on which the subjects are located.

TRANSPARENCY 8.1 cont.

Introduction   Material related to the main text of the book, which should be read before reading the rest of the book.

Letters   Personal correspondence used in a book.

Main character   Whoever is most important in the story.

Middle   Most of the action is in this part of the book, which ends with the climax of the story.

Mystery   A story that poses a problem or describes a crime and involves the reader in discovering "Who done it?"

Myth   A story to explain things in nature.

Newbery Award   An annual award given to the author of the most distinguished contribution to American children's literature published the preceding year. Established in 1921.

Novel   A quite long form of literature.

Paperback   A book with a soft cover made only of paper, to save costs in publication.

Parts of a story   Beginning, middle, end.

Plagiarism   The act of a person stealing someone's ideas and saying they are his or her own.

Play   A story written for characters to be read by individuals to entertain.

Plot   The plan for the action of a story.

Poetry   Short rhyming thoughts and inspirations.

Preface   Information about the book written by the author.

Publisher   A person or company in the business of making books for the public to read and enjoy for education and entertainment.

Recto page   The right-hand side of a page spread.

Review   Newspaper or magazine comments about the book. Sometimes called the blurb.

Scene   The place where the story takes place.

Science fiction   A highly imaginative story using actual scientific knowledge as the basis or background.

Setting   Where the story takes place.

Signatures   The folded-page sections of a book.

TRANSPARENCY 8.1 cont.

Spine   The backbone of the book. It usually shows the author's name, the title, and a label with the library's designation for fiction or nonfiction materials plus the first three letters of the author's last name.

Spine label   A sticker placed on the book by the librarian to place the book on the shelf according to the author's last name or subject.

Summary   A short description of what happens in the book.

Supporting characters   People in the story who are not the main character.

Table of contents   A list of the chapters, sections, or units of the book and the pages on which each begins.

Tall Tale   Story set in a particular region of the United States and featuring an American hero with highly exaggerated and humorous actions.

Teaser   A quick spurt of words to grab your interest and make you select the book.

Text   Words of the story.

Theme   The message of the story.

Title page   The business page of the book containing the title, author, and publisher's names. Subtitles and edition numbers may also be part of the title page.

Verso page   The left-hand side of a page spread.

Western   A book set in the American West that usually contains a great deal of action.

Fiction

Body

The **body** of a composition is usually at least three paragraphs long.

All the **body** paragraphs should have unity. This means each paragraph gives more information about the main ideas of the composition.

When **body** paragraphs flow smoothly and are in an order that makes sense, they have coherence. The **body** develops and supports the main idea statement with unity and coherence.

The **body** also includes the **introduction**, which first gets the reader's attention and states the main idea. The **conclusion** restates the main idea and leaves the reader with something to think about.

The **body** normally has a beginning, middle, and end. It presents a clear sequence of events and a consistent point of view.

Introduction

The introduction sets the stage by introducing the characters through words and actions and describing the setting.

Plot

The **plot** creates a convincing world using sensory language, concrete details, and dialogue to create believable characters and setting.

Conflict

Conflict is introduced, usually tension of some kind between characters, forming a sequence of events that propels the body of the book toward the climax.

Conclusion

The story is finished by resolving the **conflict**. The conclusion includes the last event solving the problem.

Fiction

Look for the following:

1. Message—theme
2. Style—the way the author expresses his or her ideas
3. Character construction
4. Setting and mood
5. Flashbacks
6. Subplots
7. Dialogue and dialect

Know what the following are:

8. Exposition—characters, setting, and conflict are introduced
9. Rising action—conflict and suspense build
10. Climax—conflict and tension reach a peak
11. Falling action—conflict gets worked out and tensions lessen
12. Resolution—conflict is resolved

Use a story board or some organization tool to help understand the story.

Nonfiction

In a nonfiction book, the body presents evidence that supports the thesis.

The introduction presents a thesis statement and the conclusion summarizes the ideas.

An additional component is a works cited or reference section. It is a list of the sources of information used in the body.

How to Read a Nonfiction Book

Textbook Reading

Before reading

1. Set a purpose.

    A. Preview the following.

    Title

    Headings

    Any boxed items

    Any repeated words or bold type

    Any photos, maps, graphs, charts, or diagrams, and their captions

    First and last paragraphs

    Words to know, key words,

    Topic organization, index, glossary, table of contents

    B. Read to learn. Reread. Pause and reflect.

    C. Take notes and sum up by using study cards, or make a sketch.

    D. Make a practice test. Do an activity.

    E. Remember.

Reading

1. Preview.

2. Skim the pages.

3. Read the chapter title, introduction, and conclusion for an overview.

4. Note any subheadings, key words and phrases, pronunciation guides, and margin information.

5. Read the questions at the end of the chapter to give you an idea of the information you'll need to learn.

6. Note the maps, diagrams, and other graphics.

7. Read actively, examine, interpret, and review.

8. Take notes.

9. Read critically.

10. Highlight facts and statistics.

11. Make comparisons and contrasts.

12. Use first-hand experience or examples.

13. Look for opinions of experts.

14. Research results.

15. Use logical reasoning told in chronological or time order.

16. Don't be swayed by appeals to emotion.

17. Avoid jargon or slanted biases.

Newspaper Article

1. Look at the lead.

2. Read most important details, then less important, to least important.

Magazines

1. Look at title and author.

2. Look at photographs, illustrations, and captions.

3. Look at headings and large type.

4. Look at the first paragraph.

5. Look at the general length or number of pages.

Building a Story

A story is a **narrative.** The writer uses his imagination. Every story has a **beginning**, a **middle**, and an **end**. There is a sequence of events called a plot. Most **plots** revolve around a problem that is solved at the end of the story.

Here are some suggestions to help you write a good story.

1. Begin with a sentence to grab the reader's attention.

2. Get the reader into the story in the first paragraph.

3. Create a story that entertains or makes an impression on the reader.

4. Develop a plot with a strong beginning, middle, and end.

5. Design scenes that advance the plot and are essential to the story.

6. Build characters by showing rather then telling the reader what they are like.

7. Make interesting characters that support the plot.

8. Use dialogue that reveals information about the characters.

9. Define the story setting.

10. Create conflicts with tension or suspense.

11. After the climax of the story, close with a memorable ending.

12. Write a first draft and check for the length of the story and holes in the plot that need to be reworked to make sense.

Themes

Themes are the underlying messages of a news article or story. Themes are also a major part of the problem of the story. Look for the themes of fear, evil, love, goodness, and so on.

Dust Jacket

Back flap	Back cover	Spine	Front cover	Front flap

Back cover The outside cover of a book or dust jacket, with information about the book such as the teaser, summary, reviews, and awards.

Back flap The folded part of a dust jacket, containing information about the author and illustrator of the book.

Dust jacket A paper cover to protect the book. The front inside flap usually talks about the book. The back inside flap usually talks about the author. Information about the contents of the book can be seen on the back of the jacket.

Front flap The folded part of a dust jacket, which has information about the contents of the book.

Front cover The front of the dust jacket, containing the title, author and illustrator's name, and an illustration to grab the potential reader's attention.

Spine The backbone of the book. It contains the author's name, the book title, and a label with the library's designation for fiction or nonfiction materials plus the first three letters of the author's last name.

Directions:

1. Students create a dust jacket for a book they have read as a book report.

   Variation: Students can make a dust jacket for a pretend book. The student is the author and will write about him- or herself for the front flap.

2. Students display or compare finished jackets.

Spine Labels

The spines of a book contain information to locate the materials in the library. Three different rules are used to organize materials.

1. Fiction materials are organized on the shelves by the first three letters of the author's last name.

2. Biography material is located by knowing the first three letters of the subject's last name.

3. Nonfiction books are organized using the Dewey Decimal Classification System first and then by the author's last name.

Directions:

1. Students create spine labels of a favorite book.

2. Ask other students to arrange the spine labels according to the rules.

Miss Nelson **Is** **Missing**   **Harry Allard** **ALL**

Example

NAME _____   DATE _____

Cause and Effect

Directions: Read books or stories to determine the causes and effects of each. Identifying cause and effect is important as a newspaper reading tool.

Read five stories of your choice. In the space below, list the story, the cause(s), and the effect(s), and explain if the effect is positive or negative.

Title	Cause	Effect	Positive/Negative

NAME _____ DATE _____

Characters

Place the characters in the column in which they fit *best*. Some choices are better than others—give your reasoning.

Alien	Elf	President	Robot	Vampire
Astronaut	Giant	Princess	Big Foot	Ghost
Dragon	Inventor	Athlete	Explorer	Witch

Fairy Tales	Science Fiction	Biography
1.		
2.		
3.		
4.		
5.		

Write a short story using three characters—one from each column. Choose to write the story as a fairy tale, as science fiction, or as a biography. Read your story to the class.

260

LESSON 8-B

Student's Literature Genres

To the Instructor ....

Students will read many genres in their lifetime. Genres can be divided into fiction and nonfiction. Fiction genres include fantasy, realistic fiction, historical fiction, and science fiction. Poetry, myths, legends, folk tales, and the like are located in the nonfiction sections of the library. Informational literature and biographies are also located in the nonfiction sections.

Objectives ....

1. The students learn to recognize genres.
2. The students are able to locate and use books of various genres.

Materials ....

Transparency

8.5 Genre Glossary ☐ ◧ ■

Examples of various genre books

Teaching and Preparation ....

1. Familiarize students with the characteristics and location of various forms of fantasy, realistic fiction, historical fiction, and science fiction.

2. Familiarize students with the location of the poetry, myths, and folk tales in the nonfiction section of the library media center.

2. Review Internet reference.

   www.lapl.org/kidspath/booklist/rr_genre.html

Connections to the Curriculum ....

Math—Students read about mathematicians or number systems such as the Fibonacci series.

Science—Students read about inventions, inventors, planets, dinosaurs, and extinct animals. Compare science fiction to science fact.

Social studies—Students read histories or about historical fact. Compare historical fiction to historical fact. Learn about different cultures by using folklore and folk tales to describe events in the cultures' histories.

Students compare novels to their video and movie versions.

School-wide or library association reading incentive programs for most books read within a chosen genre.

Genre Glossary

Biography　The histories of individual lives described by another person, considered as a branch of literature.

Fable　A short tale to teach a moral lesson. Animals and/or inanimate objects are characters. Stories are not founded in fact. It can be about supernatural or extraordinary persons or incidents.

Fantasy　A work of fiction portraying highly imaginative characters or settings that have no counterparts in the real world. These works deal with dragons, elves, ghosts, and similar things.

Folklore　All of the unwritten traditional beliefs, legends, sayings, customs, and so on of a culture.

Folk Tale　A tale that contains legendary elements and is handed down orally among the common people. It can be a belief or story passed on traditionally and considered to be false or based on tradition.

Historical Fiction　A work based on or suggested by people and events of the past.

Informational　A work of knowledge acquired from a collection of materials such as encyclopedias, dictionaries, and volumes on particular subjects.

Legend　A nonhistorical story handed down by tradition and accepted as historical. It is related to a particular people, or group. It can also be a collection of stories.

Myth　A traditional story, usually about a hero or event. There isn't any basis of fact or a natural explanation. It can contain gods or unusual natural elements. It is imaginary and fictitious.

Poetry　Structured writing that rhymes, or has rhythm and spirit. The poet writes with great feeling on a particular subject.

Realistic Fiction　A story with a tendency to face facts and be practical rather than imaginative or visionary.

Science Fiction　Fiction of a highly imaginative or fantastic kind, typically involving some actual or projected scientific phenomenon.

Tall Tales　A story in which characters are exaggerated and have superhuman abilities, such as being able to lasso a cyclone.

 **TRANSPARENCY 8.5**

LESSON 8-C

Folklore, Myths, and Legends

To the Instructor ....

Folklore, myths, and legends are a good way to compare people of the world and how they are diverse yet also have commonalities in their beliefs.

Objectives ....

1. Students learn that although folklore, myths, and legends are fiction, they are located in the nonfiction section 398.2 because of their social connections.

2. Students learn to recognize the characteristics of various kinds of folklore.

3. Students learn how to compare and contrast cultures using folklore.

Materials ....

Transparency

8.6 Nonfiction Fable Table ☐ ◧ ■

Folklore, myths, and legends books
Folklore, myths, and legends videos
Maps locating folklore, myths, and legends stories

Teaching and Preparation ....

1. Familiarize students with the characteristics and location of various forms of folklore in the nonfiction section of the library media center.

2. Demonstrate more folklore stories on the Internet.

3. Using folklore titles, demonstrate the sharing of ideas from different cultures.

4. Read, tell, or show videos of several short folklore stories and look for their characteristics using the chart in Transparency 8.6.

5. Have students compare and contrast heroes or heroines.

6. Review Internet references.

   http://www.yahooligans.com/School_Bell/Social_Studies/Mythology_and_Folklore

   directory.google.com/Top/Arts/Literature/Myths_and_Folktales/Myths/Directories

Activities ....

Students play the "Gossip Game" to illustrate the oral tradition of folklore. The teacher whispers a phrase or sentence to a student in a circle who whispers the phrase to the next student, and so on. The last student says the phrase out loud, and the class can see how it has changed. (no page) □ ◧ ■

Read myths and have students make up their own to explain things in nature. (no page) □ ◧ ■

Students illustrate a myth. (no page) □ ◧ ■

Connections to the Curriculum ....

Language arts—Students write folklore stories. Stories will be placed on a bulletin board in the library media center or have a check-out corner for the original stories.

Social studies—Students locate the geographic locations of folk heroes and make maps with pictures of the folk heroes.

Art—Students make puppets or dioramas.

Students could videotape and/or participate in short folklore stories for younger students or their parents at open houses or for future class viewing.

Nonfiction Fable Table

Nonfiction	398.2	398.2		398.2
Folklore	Fables	Tall Tales	Myths and Legends	Folk Tales
	Fiction	Fiction	Fiction	Fiction
Length	Brief			
Characters	Animals, plants, or things that talk	Exceptional strength, skills, or determination	Main character possesses a hero's characteristics	
Moral	Lessons stated at end; clearly states right or wrong		Evil character displays cowardice, greed, or cruelty	
Style		Exaggerated	Overtones may be religious	
				Oral Tradition

TRANSPARENCY 8.6

LESSON 8-D

Fables, Tall Tales, and Folk Tales

To the Instructor ....

Fables, tall tales, and folk tales are used to explain how things in nature happened. They can compare people of the world, and how they are diverse yet also have commonalities in their beliefs. Tall tales are about common people who are bigger and better at their jobs than ordinary people. The stories exaggerate their everyday lives.

Objectives ....

1. Students learn that although fables, tall tales, and folk tales are fiction, they are located in the nonfiction section 398.2 because of their social connections.

2. Students learn to recognize the characteristics of various kinds of folk tales and tall tales, such as those about Febold Fefoldson, Paul Bunyan, Johnny Appleseed, Pecos Bill, Casey Jones, Stormalong, John Henry, Joe Magarac, and Mike Fink.

3. Students learn how to compare and contrast cultures using folk tales.

4. Students respond to fables, tall tales, and folk tales by developing puppets, plays, and so on.

Materials ....

Transparency

8.6 Nonfiction Fable Table (previous lesson) □ ◧ ■

Fable, tall tale, and folk tale books
Fable, tall tale, and folk tale videos
Maps locating characters and stories

Teaching and Preparation ....

1. Familiarize students with the characteristics of fables, tall tales, and folk tales and their location in the nonfiction section of the library media center.

2. Demonstrate more stories on the Internet.

3. Using fables, tall tales, or folk tales, demonstrate the sharing of ideas from different cultures.

4. Read, tell, or show videos of several short stories and look for their characteristics using Transparency 8.6.

5. Have students compare and contrast heroes or heroines.

6. Review Internet references.

   http://www.yahooligans.com/School_Bell/Social_Studies/Mythology_and_Folklore

   http://home.freeuk.net/elloughton13/theatre.htm

   http://www.ucalgary.ca/~dkbrown/storfolk.html

Activities ....

Students play the "Gossip Game" to illustrate the oral tradition of folklore. The teacher whispers a phrase or sentence to a student in a circle who whispers the phrase to the next student, and so on. The last student says the phrase out loud, and the class can see how it has changed. (no page) □ ◧ ■

Share fables, tall tales, and folk tales through role playing or by using puppets. (no page) □ ◧ ■

Connections to the Curriculum ....

Language arts—Students write fables, tall tales, or folk tales. Stories will be placed on a bulletin board in the library media center or have a check-out corner for the original stories.

Social studies—Students locate the geographic locations of folk heroes and make maps with pictures of the folk heroes.

Art—Students make puppets or dioramas.

Students could videotape and/or participate in short folklore stories for younger students or their parents at open houses or for future class viewing.

LESSON 8-E

Poetry

To the Instructor ....

Poetry is written to express feelings.

Objectives ....

1. Students learn about the different kinds of poems.

2. Students learn how to write different kinds of poems.

Materials ....

Transparency

8.7 Poetry Glossary ☐ ◨ ■

Books with different kinds of poetry

Teaching and Preparation ....

1. Discuss the different kinds of poetry.

2. Display books with different kinds of poetry.

3. Read different kinds of poetry.

4. Review Internet references.

   http://www.poeticbyway.com/glossary.html (glossary of poetic terms)

   www.poems.com

   www.emule.com/poetry/

   www.poetrymagazine.org

   http://teacher.scholastic.com/writewit/poetry/index.htm

   www.veeceet.com

Activity . . . .

8.3 Activities with Poetry □ ◧ ■

Connections to the Curriculum . . . .

Collaboration with the language arts teacher is a must. The language arts teacher should reinforce the skills and books.

Poetry Glossary

Alliteration   Repeating the same sound at the beginning of words that are near one another.

Assonance   Repeating the same vowel sound several times in a piece of writing.

Blank verse   A nonrhyming, metered poem.

Concrete poem   Poem in which its shape reflects its content.

Couplet   Two lines that usually share the rhythm and rhyme.

Free verse   A nonrhyming poem that does not have a pattern.

Haiku   A poem three lines long that does not rhyme. The first line must have five syllables, the second line seven, and the last one five again.

Limerick   A poem five lines long, and usually funny. The first, second, and fifth lines have three strong beats each and all rhyme with one another. The third and fourth lines are shorter. They have two strong beats each, and they rhyme with each other.

Metaphor   Describing something as if it were something else.

Onomatopoeia   Words that sound like what they mean.

Personification   Describing something that is not human in terms we use to describe people.

Similes   Describing something by comparing it to something else, using "like" or "as."

Sonnet   A fourteen-line poem with a fixed rhyme scheme.

 **TRANSPARENCY 8.7**

Activities with Poetry

Theme—Friendship

1. Each student writes one sentence describing what a friend is. Combine the sentences to form a single poem.

Theme—Feelings

2. Students draw their feelings and share or compare with others.

Theme—Riddle poetry

3. Students try to "stump" their classmates with their own poetic riddles.

Collaboration skills

4. Students do the following:

    Read poems to partners

    Include their names as part of poems

    Make jump rope rhymes

    Act out poems (one student reads while the other one acts)

    In pairs, use only illustrations to tell each other a poem or story

    Create a picture together

    Invent new words

    Create a class book of poetry

    Work in small groups to write new stanzas for old poems

    Create onomatopoeia word lists

The "Magic Bag"

Place various objects in a paper or cloth bag. Students put their hands into the bag and then describe in rhyme what they touch.

Valentine's Day Project

Students select scenes from favorite books and poems and make placemat sets to donate to hospitals and retirement homes.

LESSON 8-F

Award Winners

To the Instructor

How can a student find a good book to read? Reliable suggestions may be found in the lists of award-winning books.

Objective

Students are introduced to good literature by reading books from award-winning book lists.

Materials

Transparency

8.8 Award Winners ☐ ◧ ■

Posters of Caldecott, Newbery, and other award-winning books

Teaching and Preparation

1. Distribute lists of award-winning books.

2. Read excerpts from award-winning books to encourage further reading.

3. Use the Internet to find lists of Caldecott, Newbery, and other award-winning books.

4. Review Internet references.

   http://www.yahooligans.com/School_Bell/language_arts/Book_ Awards/

   http://www.ala.org/alsc/cquick.html (Caldecott Winners 1938–2003)

   http://www.ala.org/alsc/nquick.html (Newbery Winners 1922–2003)

Worksheet . . . .

8.3 Checking the Firsts ☐ ◨ ■

Connections to the Curriculum . . . .

Students should always choose quality books.

Answer Key . . . .

WORKSHEET 8.3

1. Bookseller
2. *The Story of Mankind*
3. Hendrik Wilhelm von Loon
4. 1922
5. Illustrator
6. *Animals of the Bible: A Picture Book*
7. Dorothy P. Lathrop
8. 1938

Award Winners

The Randolph Caldecott Medal

The Caldecott Medal was named in honor of nineteenth-century English illustrator Randolph Caldecott. It is awarded annually by the Association for Library Service to Children, a division of the American Library Association, to the artist of the most distinguished American picture book for children.

Frederic G. Melcher suggested this award in 1937, because the Newbery Medal was given for the best literature, and he felt that artists' contributions to books should also be recognized.

The Coretta Scott King Award

The Coretta Scott King Award is presented annually by the Coretta Scott King Task Force of the American Library Association's Social Responsibilities Round Table. Recipients are authors and illustrators of African descent whose distinguished books promote an understanding and appreciation of the "American Dream."

The award commemorates the life and work of Dr. Martin Luther King Jr., and honors his widow, Coretta Scott King, for her courage and determination in continuing the work for peace and world brotherhood.

The John Newbery Medal

The Newbery Medal is named for the eighteenth-century English bookseller. It is awarded annually by the American Library Association for the most distinguished American children's book published the previous year.

Frederic G. Melcher proposed the award in 1921.

Checking the Firsts

Directions: Access the following site and answer the questions below: (http://www.yahooligans.com/school_bell/language_arts/Book_Awards/).

1. Who was John Newbery?

2. What is the name of the book that won the first Newbery Medal?

3. Who was the author of this book?

4. In what year was this book awarded the medal?

5. Who was Randolph Caldecott?

6. What was the name of the book that won the first Caldecott Medal?

7. Who was the illustrator of the book?

8. In what year was the book awarded the medal?

Book Reports

To the Instructor

What is the purpose of reading? We read to be entertained or informed. Students should be able to show teachers that they have understood what they have read. Book reports may be done in numerous ways. No one way is the best.

Objectives

1. Students learn how to inform others about the book, article, or story they have read.
2. Students learn how to put their information into a format for presentation.

Materials

Book lists, books, or magazines

Teaching and Preparation

1. Review the concept of story, theme, characters, setting, and plot.
2. Study the beginnings, middles, and ends of stories and personal writing.

3. Use simple stories like "The Three Little Pigs" for a sample book report.

4. Review Internet references.

www.homeworkspot.com/features/bookreports.htm

www.teachnet.com/lesson/langarts/reading/bookrepts1.html

www.geniuspapers.com

Worksheets ....

8.4 Book Report Planning Sheet ☐ ◧ ■

8.5 Fairy Tale Headlines ☐ ◧

8.6 History Book Report ◧ ■

Connections to the Curriculum ....

All subject areas have students read and report in some way their understanding of the material.

Answer Key ....

WORKSHEETS 8.4 AND 8.6

Answers will vary.

WORKSHEET 8.5

Cinderella
The Three Little Pigs
Pinocchio

Book Report Planning Sheet

Directions: Use this form to help prepare your book report.

1. Read to remember from cover to cover.

2. Fill out bibliography information for the book.

3. Type (genre) of literature, and theme: _____

4. Story setting—place and time: _____

5. Plot: _____

6. Story characters

   A. Main characters: _____

   _____

   B. Supporting characters: _____

   _____

7. Story problem: _____

8. Story action—list the events: _____

   _____

9. Story outcome—resolution to problem: _____

   _____

10. Comments—opinion of the book: _____

    _____

11. Write the final report in complete paragraphs.

12. Retell the story in your own words orally, in written form, or artistically (drawings).

NAME _____ DATE _____

Fairy Tale Headlines

Directions:

1. Write the correct title of the fairy tale described by the headlines below.

2. Write your own headline for other students to guess, and then read the story.

3. For a different kind of book report, write the story as a news article.

GIRL LOSES SHOE AT THE BALL

THREE BROTHERS LOSE THEIR HOMES

PUPPET BECOMES REAL BOY

History Book Report

Directions: Choose a time period and be a detective or reporter. Write your book report for a newspaper or magazine. Do research with reference books, encyclopedias, the Internet, and so on. Include the following questions as part of your report.

1. What year did you choose?

2. Who was president of the United States?

3. What was the population of the United States?

4. What was the most important news story of that time?

5. What war was fought closest to this time?

6. Name some of the important people of the time?

7. What did people do for fun?

8. What was a popular movie or entertainment of the time?

LESSON 8-H

Copyright

To the Instructor

Copyright is the exclusive right of the author to control the copying of his or her work. Many students in writing papers copy verbatim from books, the Internet, and other sources and do not give the author credit. This lesson is a definition of what copyright is and seeks to develop a respect for the work of other people.

Objectives

1. Students learn to recognize and respect the copyright symbol (©).

2. Students learn how to cite materials in a bibliography.

3. Students learn not to copy verbatim, but to attempt to use their own words.

Materials

Transparency

    8.9 Copyright Laws and Rules □ ◧ ■

Materials displaying the copyright symbol
Bibliography reference sheet
Online computer

Teaching and Preparation ....

1. Display copyright symbols in books and other materials.

2. Distribute a copy of Worksheet 8.6 for student use.

Activities ....

Students locate the copyright symbol in print materials such as books, maps, graphics, and so on. (no page) ☐ ◩ ■

Students access sites on the Internet that grant permission to copy and those that give restrictions. (no page) ☐ ◩ ■

Worksheet ....

8.7 Checking Copyright ☐ ◩ ■

Connections to the Curriculum ....

All curriculum areas use materials that are copyrighted. Students need to know how to give credit to the author.

Answer Key ....

WORKSHEET 8.7

Answers will vary.

Copyright Laws and Rules

Copyrighted material must exist in some tangible form.

The material has to be creative.

Nothing done by the U.S. government can be copyrighted inside the United States.

The copyright owner can sell some rights to his copyright.

You must comply with the wishes of the authors on the Internet.

The "fair use" doctrine exists to stop copyright law from being used to stifle criticism and academia.

The Berne copyright convention, which almost all major nations have signed, states that every creative work is copyrighted the instant it is fixed in material form. No registration is necessary.

The copyright lasts until fifty years after the author dies.

Facts and ideas can't be copyrighted.

Fonts as printed on paper cannot be copyrighted.

The correct form for a notice is:
     "copyright [dates] by [author/owner]"

The phrase "All Rights Reserved" used to be required in some nations but it is not needed now.

The owner must put software or Internet sites into public domain by saying "I grant this to the public domain" to release all rights.

If you write a story using someone else's characters, you must get permission from that author or producer.

In parody, making fun of someone else or the person's material doesn't need that person's permission.

Copyright law is civil law.

Copyright is violated whether you are charged money or not.

The Digital Millennium Copyright Act has amended copyright law on the Internet.

Computers are given commands, not permission. Only people can be given permission.

The U.S. Library of Congress is a copyright site.

 **TRANSPARENCY 8.9**

NAME _____   DATE _____

Checking Copyright

Directions:

Locate and write the title and copyright information for each of the following materials.

1. Language arts textbook: _____

2. Children's magazine: _____

3. Software program: _____

4. Video, CD, or DVD: _____

5. Encyclopedia: _____

6. Television program: _____

7. What does the copyright symbol look like? _____

8. Where is the copyright symbol found in a book, a magazine, a video, and a software program?

_____

_____

_____

_____

UNIT
NINE

Electronic Materials

Videotapes, CDs, DVDs, and Audiotapes

To the Instructor

Today students can "read" a book in many different formats other than the printed page. The Internet has complete books to read online or to download. Videotape, CD, DVD, and audiotape adaptations are also available.

Objective

Students learn how to compare a book in print to a videotape and/or audiotape version.

Materials

Fiction books that have a videotape or audiotape version available for comparison

Teaching and Preparation

1. Read a short book that has a videotape or audiotape version in the library media center.

2. Show the video and/or listen to the audiotape version of the book. Compare how the versions are similar and different.

Activities . . . .

Students read print versions of books that have a videotape or audiotape version. (no page) ☐ ◨ ■

Students view or listen to the tape versions then write a comparison of the different versions. (no page) ☐ ◨ ■

Students read and tape a short book for the library media center's electronic collection. (no page) ☐ ◨ ■

Worksheets . . . .

9.1 Closed Captioning ☐ ◨ ■

9.2 Which Is Better? ☐ ◨ ■

9.3 Music, Music, Music ☐ ◨ ■

Connections to the Curriculum . . . .

This activity will strengthen reading and language arts skills. Students will learn to compare and contrast materials.

Answer Key . . . .

WORKSHEET 9.1

1. No. It is expensive, and is not needed for the average user.
2. Closed captioning on foreign films is for translation, or to see the words to study the language.
3. Persons who are hearing impaired need closed captioning. Persons studying languages can also use captioning.
4. Food, cooking, gardening, exercise, and sports are some videos that do not need closed captioning for the *average* viewer.
5. Copyright information is on the outside case or container for the tape, DVD, or CD, as well as at the beginning or end of the tape itself.
6. CDs can also contain software games or recorded books.
7. Answers will vary.
8. Answers will vary.

WORKSHEET 9.2

1. An exercise videotape would be better, because you could see the actual movements.
2. An opera on videotape would show the costumes, and could have closed captioning of the language or the translation.
3. A cookbook in print would be better because you use it in the kitchen and need the ingredients list in front of you while you are preparing the food.
4. Always read the book. Videos of a book do not always follow the printed word. If you are an audio learner, and the book has been read for sight-impaired people, the book will be accurate.
5. If you need pictures, it is best to use a photocopy of a picture in print, as that would be the easiest to reproduce on a written work.
6. All three would be useful, as you would benefit from all three forms.

WORKSHEET 9.3

1. Classical, folk, hymns, jazz, movie, opera, popular, and so on are some kinds of music to be found on CDs.
2. No. CDs can be used for software games. CDs and audiotapes may be recordings of books.
3. Electronic materials are in their own section and grouped as music (classical, folk, and so on); software; or books on tape.
4. Answers will vary.
5. You are requested to rewind the tape for the next user.
6. No. CDs, DVDs, videotapes, and audiotapes are copyrighted.

Closed Captioning

Directions: Use the electronic materials section of your library to answer the following questions.

1. Do all videos and DVDs have closed caption dialogue as part of their presentation? Why, or why not?

2. What would be a reason to have closed caption dialogue on a foreign film?

3. Who needs closed captioning, and why?

4. List some types of videos and DVDs that do not need closed captioning for the *average* audience.

5. Where do you find the copyright information on a videotape, CD, audiotape, or DVD?

6. Besides music, what are the other kinds of CDs?

7. Find a video with closed captioning and write the name here.

8. Find two different kinds of CDs and write the names here.

NAME _____ DATE _____

Which Is Better?

Directions: Use the electronic materials section of your library to answer the following questions.

1. Which would be more useful, an exercise book or an exercise videotape? Why?

2. Which would be better, an opera on videotape or on audiotape? Why?

3. Which would be more useful, a cookbook on videotape or one in print? Why?

4. Which would be best to use for a book report you need to do for an English class, a print, video, or audio version of the book? Why?

5. Which would be best to use for a written assignment that needs accompanying pictures, a print or videotape version of the pictures? Why?

6. Which would be useful for learning a second language, a printed book, a videotape, or an audiotape? Why?

Music, Music, Music

Directions: Use the electronic materials section of your library to answer the following questions.

1. Name different kinds of music that might be found on CDs and audiotapes.

2. Are CDs and audiotapes for music only? If no, what other kinds of CDs and audiotapes are in the library?

3. How are CDs and audiotapes organized in the library?

4. Does your library have special rules for borrowing electronic materials? If yes, what are the rules?

5. If you borrow video- or audiotapes, what are you requested to do?

6. Can you make copies of the electronic materials you borrow from the library? Why or why not?

LESSON 9-B

Microfiche

To the Instructor

The preservation of newspapers and magazine articles on microfiche is an important part of library services. Students should be aware of this format used by high school, university, and public libraries.

Objectives

1. Students learn why information on microfiche is important.

2. Students learn how to use a microfiche reader to find information.

Materials

Transparency

    9.1 Microfiche Glossary ■

Microfiche
Microfiche reader

Teaching and Preparation ....

1. Demonstrate how to load and read a microfiche reader.

2. Show how to locate information using the microfiche reader.

Activity ....

Students choose a historic date like their birth, or their first day at their school, and then use microfiche to find out events that happened on this date. (no page) ■

Worksheet ....

9.4 Paper to Plastic to Paper ■

Connections to the Curriculum ....

Students should be able to use newspaper and magazine articles for historical reference in all classes.

Answer Key ....

WORKSHEET 9.4

1. Important information on paper is photographed and miniaturized using microfiche film to preserve it for five hundred years or more. The microfiche film makes it easy to keep large amounts of information in very small spaces. The microfiche reader lets you view the information and then print out a paper copy to take along.
2. You cannot take a piece of film or plastic with you when you are finished viewing it.
3. Genealogical material, newspapers, magazines, government information, and statistical information are some things preserved on microfiche film.
4. People doing research for reports, family history, statistical changes, or tracking trends use microfiche.
5. Answers will vary.

Microfiche Glossary

Fiche carrier   A device on which the roll of film is threaded through rollers for viewing.

Format of microfiche   Either a 16 or 35 mm roll of microfilm, or a small piece of plastic resembling a file card in a paper envelope.

Microfiche   A roll or sheet of cellulose acetate film on which a number of reduced photocopies of newspapers or magazines can be preserved and viewed by a machine.

Microfiche reader   A retrieval system of spindles, magnifying lenses, and light.

Preservation   To keep from spoiling, rotting, or disintegrating into disuse. Microfiche has a life expectancy of five-hundred-plus years.

 **TRANSPARENCY 9.1**

NAME _____   DATE _____

Paper to Plastic to Paper

Directions: Use a microfiche reader and answer the following questions.

1. Why is the title of this sheet "Paper to Plastic to Paper"?

2. Why is it important that you are able to make copies when you use a microfiche machine?

3. What information is preserved on microfiche film?

4. Who uses microfiche?

5. Assignment

   A. Write down an important date in your life (birthday, the day you broke your arm, or something similar).

   B. Use a microfiche reader and find out three things that happened on that date. Write them here.

   C. Print the front page of the newspaper from your date.

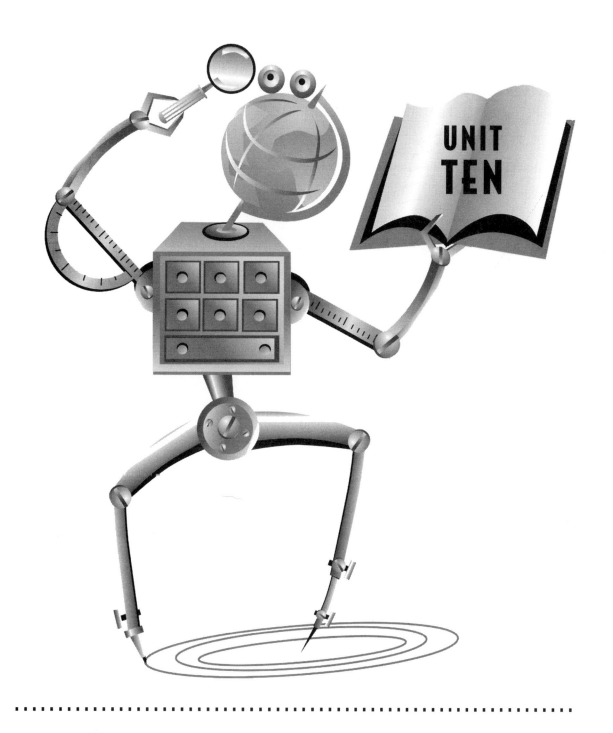

UNIT
TEN

Computers and the Internet

LESSON 10-A

Search Engines

To the Instructor

What are good sources for information on the Internet? It is important to have a few good starting points for research.

Objectives

1. Students learn how to access different search engines.

2. Students gain knowledge of the online equivalents of reference books.

3. Students learn how to improve their searching.

4. Students learn how to credit a site as part of a project.

Materials

Transparencies

10.1 Rules for Searching the Web ☐ ◧ ■

10.2 Rules for Browsing the Web ☐ ◧ ■

10.3 Search Engines and Online Information ☐ ◧ ■

Online computers
Lists of key words to practice searches

Teaching and Preparation ....

1. Demonstrate search engines that are appropriate for student use, and explain the following Web terminology.

    http = hypertext transfer protocol

    www = world wide web

    // = forward slashes

    . = dot

    : = colon

    com = commercial

    gov = government

    edu = education

    hits = times your search engine locates your key word

2. Demonstrate online reference books.

3. Have students practice locating and citing information.

Activity ....

Practice accessing search engines and online reference books. (no page) □ ◧ ■

Worksheet ....

10.1 Computer Research □ ◧ ■

Connections to the Curriculum ....

All curriculum areas use the Internet for research.

Answer Key ·

WORKSHEET 10.1

1. Type the search engine's name in the location box at the top of the screen.
2. A search engine is a tool to locate information. A Website is a single location for a subject.
3. The letters *http* stand for hypertext transfer protocol, the language an Internet computer operates with.
4. The letters *www* stand for World Wide Web, the pictures and words together of the Internet.
5. *FAQ* stands for Frequently Asked Questions, an area of a site that gives information many people have already asked about and that is kept in a databank.
6. A key word is the subject you are trying to find information about using the Internet.
7. The abbreviations *com* stands for commercial, *gov* stands for government, and *edu* stands for education. These tell what kind of institution the site is from.
8. Hits are the number of times your search engine is able to locate the use of your key word in Websites on the Internet. Hits are also the number of times a particular Website has been accessed.
9. "Case sensitive" means that whether a letter is capitalized or not capitalized can affect the Internet searching of that search engine.
10. The "back" button will return your computer to the previous screen or site.
11. Answers will vary.
12. Answers will vary.

Rules for Searching the Web

1. Check your spelling and typing when entering information.

2. Don't type plurals.

3. Remember that some entries are case sensitive.

4. Use synonyms and variations of your key words.

5. Remember that "hits" appear in a relevancy ranking.

6. Remember that some information on the Internet is copyrighted and will not download.

7. Keep track of your sites as you surf or use the back button to return to the previous site.

8. Don't use commonly occurring articles "a,""an,""in""on" and verbs "be,""is,""are."

9. Do use Boolean Operators "and,""or,""both."

10. Bookmark sites you visit frequently.

11. Read the FAQs (frequently asked questions).

12. Learn what frequently used abbreviations mean:

    a. http = hyper text transfer protocol

    b. www = world wide web

    c. // = forward slashes

    d. . = dot

    e. : = colon

    f. com = commercial

    g. gov = government

    h. edu = education

    i. hits = times your search engine locates your key word

Rules for Browsing the Web

1. Be sure you ask permission to use the online computers, and log on if your library or school requires it.

2. Type the address of the search engine you will use in the browser's window.

3. Have ready all the information and questions you have developed.

4. Type your key words in the window of your search engine.

5. Limit your searches by using Boolean Logic word phrases including quotation marks and the words "and,""or,""not."

6. If you have problems getting "hits," check your spelling and typing.

7. If you find any questionable sites, be sure to notify the instructor on duty.

8. Look for the document source of your sites to prove you have chosen good resources to prove your points.

9. Do not e-mail or give any personal information to anyone while working on any reports.

 **TRANSPARENCY 10.2**

Search Engines and Online Information

Search Engines

Alta Vista	http://www.altavista.digital.com
Ask Jeeves	http://www.ajkids.com
DogPile	http://www.dogpile.com
Excite	http://www.excite.com
Google	http://www.google.com
HotBot	http://www.hotbot.com
Infoseek	http://www.infoseek.com
Lycos	http://www.lycos.com
WebCrawler	http://www.webcrawler.com
Yahoo	http://www.yahoo.com
Yahooligans	http://www.yahooligans.com

Online Information

Almanac	http://www.almanac.com
Atlas	http://nationalgeographic.com
	http://www.infospace.com
Bartlett's Quotations	http://www.cc.columbia.edu
Biographical dictionary	http://www.s9.com
Dictionary	http://www.m-w.com
Encyclopedia	http://www.encyclopedia.com
Newspaper	http://www.usatoday.com
Research	http://www.exploratorium.edu
Thesaurus	http://www.m-w.com
Library of Congress	http://www.loc.gov
State information	http://www.state.MO.us (This is for the state of Missouri. Change "MO" to your state's abbreviation.)
House of Representatives	http://www.house.gov
Senate	http://www.senate.gov

 **TRANSPARENCY 10.3**

NAME _____   DATE _____

Computer Research

1. How do you access a search engine?

2. What is the difference between a search engine and a Website?

3. What do the letters *http* stand for?

4. What do the letters *www* stand for?

5. What do the letters *FAQ* stand for?

6. What is a key word?

7. What do the abbreviations *com, gov,* and *edu* stand for?

8. What are hits?

9. What does "case sensitive" mean?

10. What does the "back" button do?

11. Go to http://www.google.com. Pick a key word from one of your current courses of study. What key word did you choose? How many hits did you find for it?

12. Go to http://www.almanac.com. What day of the week will Lincoln's birthday fall on this year?

Remember to keep a record of your search.

Using the Internet

To the Instructor

This lesson is for showing students how to use the Internet to access information. It gives helpful hints for successful searching. It is the instructor's responsibility to keep the students on task and safe from sites that are not suitable for them. Students must realize that not all the information on the Internet is authored by experts. Some sites will be gone when the students try to revisit.

Objectives

1. Students learn how to use the browser search engines to acquire information for their projects.

2. Students learn to cite the Websites they have located.

3. Students learn to follow the rules for using computers.

4. Students learn to record the sites for future use.

Materials

A list of key words and questions developed for research
Student handbook pages for recording nonprint Internet research
Online computer

Teaching and Preparation . . . .

1. Have students practice typing Web addresses and the names of various search engines in the URL/location box window of the browser.

2. Demonstrate how to use the "back" button to return to the home screen and explain that the button is a safe way to exit sites that are questionable.

3. Have students compare the search engines and decide which ones they feel are more geared to their age groups.

4. Demonstrate how to conduct a key word search. Success in locating a key word through the search engine is called a "hit."

5. Show students that hits are ranked according to the greatest relevancy or the most times they appear in an article.

6. Demonstrate that Boolean Logic can increase the number of hits by phrasing words in quotation marks with the words "and," "or," "not" used in the phrase. Example: "cats not wild cats"

7. Have students evaluate their information and look for the document source to evaluate the site's information.

8. Students will use hypertext links (different colored words and pictures) to search related sites.

9. Show students how to "bookmark" good sites for their project. (Bookmarks are part of the browser program, sometimes called "Favorites.") Some schools or libraries may not allow bookmarks because they take up computer memory, and because other students need to be able to access sites on their own.

Activities . . . .

Students locate sources to answer key word searches. (no page) ☐ ◨ ■

Students will cite the sites correctly. (no page) ☐ ◨ ■

Connections to the Curriculum . . . .

Everything and every subject can be found on the Internet. Some sites are very commercial, and others are cluttered and difficult to use. The Internet is very valuable for its up-to-date information, as long as you are critical and make sure the sites you review are completely accurate and friendly.

LESSON 10-C

Electronic Reference Software

To the Instructor ....

What is an alternative to print and the Internet for reference materials? Do all of your students have Internet access on home computers? Some students will need reference software to answer their research questions.

Objectives ....

1. Students learn how to evaluate reference software.

2. Students learn how to use reference software for research information.

Materials ....

Reference software (National Geographic CD-ROM, CD-ROMS on animals, art, plants, inventions)

Teaching and Preparation ....

1. Compare print materials, the Internet, and reference software on the same subject.

2. Discuss how to cite information from software, and what may and may not be copied for personal use.

Activities..

Students research the same topic using various reference sources
(the Internet, reference software, an encyclopedia, a book on the subject).
(no page) □ ◧ ■

Students list advantages and disadvantages of using reference software.
(no page) □ ◧ ■

Connections to the Curriculum ....

Many different topics are available in reference software. Curriculum teachers may want
to have specific titles on hand to keep the students on task, and to have consistent
results to questions.

LESSON 10-D

Word Processing

To the Instructor

Are you familiar with the vocabulary of word processing? The different programs all perform about the same. Word processing is an integral part of the language arts program.

Objectives

1. Students learn how to use a word processing program to type their projects.
2. Students perfect tool bar skills to change fonts, size, and so on.

Materials

Transparency

    10.4 Word Processing Glossary □ ◨ ■

Instructional computer with word processing software

Teaching and Preparation . . . .

1. Type a sign or short sentence.

2. Show how to change fonts and other tools.

3. Practice spell checking, proofreading, and printing.

Activities . . . .

Students design a travel brochure for a country studied in social studies class. (no page) □ ◨ ■

Encourage students to cultivate pen pals, either by snail mail or e-mail. (no page) □ ◨ ■

Students produce a school or class newspaper. (no page) □ ◨ ■

Students type one or more of the following: coupons or cards as gifts to parents for occasions; book reports; poetry. (no page) □ ◨ ■

Connections to the Curriculum . . . .

The computer specialist will collaborate with the librarian to produce reports for all subject areas.

Word Processing Glossary

Bold, italics, and underscore   Ways to emphasize a printed word.

Clipboard   The section of your computer's hard drive which holds information that has been cut or copied from a document. You may import from a clipboard to a document. This information may be words or pictures.

Copy   Computer function that allows you to type something one time, highlight the area, and command the computer to reproduce it many times.

Delete   To remove entire documents or sections of a document. To delete, press the backspace key or the delete key, or highlight text and use "cut" from the edit menu.

Desk top   The initial or main screen on your computer that shows the icons of the programs on your computer's hard drive.

Disk   Magnetic piece of round plastic capable of storing information from a computer.

Document   The name of all typed materials, such as stories and reports, in a word processing program.

Fonts   Different types of letter design.

Hard copy   The paper copy of the document that is viewed on the computer screen.

Hard drive   The memory portion of a computer on which all the programs and documents are saved.

Highlight   Selecting a word or group of words. You highlight by holding the mouse button down and drawing it over material in your document. The area is a negative to the rest of the work. You can cut, delete, copy, spell check, and language check highlighted words. Click the mouse button anywhere on your document to remove the highlighting.

Insert   The computer command that tells the program to bring in information from the clipboard, the desktop, or another file. This is commonly used when you are importing information from the Internet. You may also place page breaks, footnotes, captions, and pictures from the menu bar.

Internet   A system that links your computer via telephone or ISDN lines to computers all over the world.

 TRANSPARENCY 10.4

Menu bar   The display, usually at the top of the computer screen, with pull-down windows that allow you to edit, insert, spell check, and so on.

Move   A computer function that lets you cut, copy, or paste information within the document by using the edit options of your program.

Print   To reproduce your document on hard copy (paper).

Replace   A computer function that substitutes or adds to the document you are working on.

Retrieve   The process of calling up a saved document from the computer's memory or an external disk.

Save   To record a document for future use. There are two ways to save documents, onto the computer's hard drive and onto a separate disk. Important documents should be saved both ways to ensure that they will not be lost. Another way to save a document is to print a hard copy.

Scroll   Computer function that allows you to use the arrow keys or side scroll bar to move up and down through your document.

Spell check   Computer program that checks for spelling mistakes as you type. It checks the spelling against a built-in dictionary.

Word processing   Using a computer program to write, edit, and print stories and reports.

Word wrap   The continuation of type onto the next line when there is no more room on the first line. You do not have to press the return key until you are ready to begin a new paragraph.

LESSON 10-E

Production Software

To the Instructor

HyperStudio,™ Kid Pix,™ and PowerPoint™ are registered production software programs.

Objective

Students will become familiar with software that will allow them to do presentations using a computer.

Materials

Transparencies

10.5 HyperStudio ◧ ■

10.6 Kid Pix □ ◧ ■

10.7 PowerPoint ■

Computer with production software: HyperStudio, Kid Pix, and PowerPoint

Teaching and Preparation ....

1. Demonstrate production software.

Activity ....

10.1 Practice Procedures ☐ ◨ ■

Connections to the Curriculum ....

All subject areas use production software to demonstrate in an interesting manner what the student has learned. Teachers also use PowerPoint.

HyperStudio

HyperStudio is production software that allows the user to combine graphics, text, and sound to create slide shows of information. Students can create their own artwork and text and also do animation.

About this stack   Provides information about the entire stack. Pull down from the Objects menu.

Actions   Things to do. Play a sound, movie, animation, or video.

BlabberMouth   The computer will read the text aloud.

Buttons   The basic way that users move through stacks and activate multimedia elements such as sound, video, animation, and other actions.

Card   The basic program element. Each individual screen within a stack is called a card.

Clip art   Graphic images from another source such as a disk or the Internet.

Cookie cutter effect   The process of selecting an area of a card, "cutting" a pattern from another piece of artwork, and using it in your show.

Digital camera   A computerized camera that you can connect to your computer to add pictures to your "show."

Edit   Cut (delete), copy, and paste text and graphics.

Group card   A card designated as part of a group. Cards in a group can share backgrounds and objects.

Home stack   The folder as the application first starts up.

Hypertext   Words that, when clicked on, cause some kind of action to occur. They can link the program to the Internet.

Marked card   A card "tagged" so that a button using the "Places to Go" action called "Last Marked Card" will move the user to the last marked card visited, even if it is in a different stack.

Plug-ins   The use of programs such as Adobe Photoshop as part of your presentation.

Scale and rotate   To flip an image sideways.

Slide show   A continuous display of the cards in your stack.

Stack   A file that contains one or more cards, along with any buttons, graphics, sounds, and other multimedia elements that have been placed on those cards.

Storyboard   Lets you see all the cards you have created. You can rearrange or delete cards here.

Transition   A visual effect when moving from one card to the next.

TRANSPARENCY 10.5

Kid Pix

Kid Pix is production software for younger students. It is more oriented to casual presentations, and students as young as three years of age can use it to draw or import pictures and create slide shows. The drawing area is like a blank sheet of paper, and the drawing screen has tools displayed on the left side of the screen. Kid Pix has sound effects, plus it lets the user record a spoken message. The user can also import pictures from clip art to digitized photos. The program can change the printed directions from English to Spanish. Kid Pix allows the instructor to combine individual work into a presentation.

Kid Pix Terms

Electric mixer   An effect that changes your drawings and mixes them up, such as changing black to white, and so on.

Scrapbook   Stored images to use in a Kid Pix presentation.

Small Kids   A feature that makes parts of the menu bar disappear so that children will not choose them accidentally.

Wacky Brush   A tool that paints in a variety of ways.

Wacky Pencil   A tool that draws free-form lines.

PowerPoint

PowerPoint is part of the Microsoft Office suite of computer programs. It has the standard cut, copy, and paste commands, but instead of making documents the user is making presentations similar to slide shows. Presentations can be printed on 35mm slides for a fee.

Bullet   An accent character to draw attention to a series of paragraphs.

Collapse an outline   Change a slide so that only the slide titles are shown.

Expand an outline   Restore the collapsed text body.

Notes   Attachments to slides that don't appear on the slides themselves but are displayed separately.

Office clipboard   Lets the user gather up to twenty-four items of text or graphics from any Office program and paste into another document.

Outline   The titles and body text of each slide, viewed to the left of the production panel.

Output   On-screen presentation, Web presentation, black and white overheads, color overheads, and 35mm slides.

Page up and Page down   Command to move the presentation backward or forward to different slides.

Placeholder   An area on a slide that it is reserved for text, clip art, a graph, or some other type of object. There are two placeholders on each slide: one for text objects, one for the title and the subtitle.

Promoting or demoting paragraphs   Moving paragraphs up one level or down one level in the outline.

Slide sorter   Screen in which all the slides are viewed at the same time, allowing you to move a slide by clicking and dragging it to a new location.

Status bar   Graphic at the very bottom of the screen that tells you which slide is currently displayed.

Task pane   Window to the right of the slide area in which options to create are displayed.

Practice Procedures

Directions: Students create their own presentation by following these instructions. They may use any of the three production software programs to complete their presentations.

1. Choose a familiar story—The Three Little Pigs, Goldilocks and the Three Bears, or something similar. Develop a story outline of two or three lines.

2. Type this outline using production software.

3. Add appropriate pictures and graphics.

4. Experiment with the different tools.

   A. Type a topic line.

   B. Type two or three subtopic lines.

   C. Add "bullets" to subtopic lines.

   D. Add graphics, sound, transitions, and so on.

5. Present shows.

UNIT ELEVEN

Using What You Have Learned: Writing and Publishing

LESSON 11-A

Organizational Systems

To the Instructor

Do students know how many ways the resources in the library are organized? Materials in the library media center are organized alphabetically, numerically, chronologically, and topically by subject.

Objectives

1. Students gain knowledge of the organizational systems of the library media center.

2. Students learn how to locate materials using the organizational systems of the library media center.

Materials

Transparency

11.1 Library Media Center Organizational Systems ☐ ◧ ■

Sample materials from the library media center to demonstrate the organizational systems

Teaching and Preparation ....

1. Describe the library organizational systems.

2. Display and discuss representative materials from the library shelves.

Worksheet ....

11.1 Find the Organizational System □ ◨ ■

Connections to the Curriculum ....

Art—artist and products information
Language arts—novels, how-to's
Math—math games
Music—recording of Mozart
Physical education—athletic records
Science—*National Geographic* article about ants
Social studies—video of prehistoric animals

Answer Key ....

WORKSHEET 11.1

1. A	6. A	10. C
2. C	7. C	11. B
3. A	8. D	12. A
4. A	9. A	13. C
5. A		

Resources could have more than one correct answer. These answers are the first organizational element.

Library Media Center Organizational Systems

FICTION

Alphabetical

Author's last name

Title (A, An, The)

Subject

Numerical

Chronological

Historical fiction

Subject

Alphabetical

REFERENCE

Alphabetical

Title (A, An, The)

Subject

Material (almanac, atlas, and so on)

Numerical

Dewey Decimal classification

Chronological

Historical sequence

Subject

Alphabetical

NONFICTION

Alphabetical

Author's last name

Title (A, An, The)

Subject

Numerical

Dewey Decimal classification

Chronological

Historical sequence

Subject

Alphabetical

BIOGRAPHY

Alphabetical

Title (A, An, The)

Person—Last name, first name

Numerical

92—Biography

920—Group biography

Chronological

Time sequence

Subject

Alphabetical

TRANSPARENCY 11.1

Find the Organizational System

Each section of the library media center (fiction, nonfiction, reference, and biography) is further divided into the following: **chronological** (order in time), **numerical** (number order), **alphabetical** (letter order), and **topical** (subject order).

Directions: Write the letter for the organizational system that best describes how to use the resource.

A = Alphabetical   B = Chronological   C = Numerical   D = Topical

_____   1. Atlas

_____   2. Biography section

_____   3. Book index

_____   4. Dictionary

_____   5. Encyclopedia

_____   6. Fiction section

_____   7. Nonfiction section

_____   8. Reference section

_____   9. *Reader's Guide*

_____ 10. Table of contents

_____ 11. Almanac

_____ 12. Thesaurus

_____ 13. Dewey Classification System

Self-Organization

To the Instructor

Where do students get started? What are they supposed to do? Students must organize their ideas, materials, and resources to be able to get started and get finished.

Objectives

1. Students learn how to keep track of important papers and information.

2. Students learn the skills to put together reports and projects.

Materials

Transparency

11.2 Self-Organization Checklist ☐ ◧ ■

Sample materials from the library media center to demonstrate how to organize ideas

Teaching and Preparation ....

1. Provide the students with pages to help organize ideas.
2. Do a sample project with students.

Connections to the Curriculum ....

All assignments for every subject area need organization for successful results.

Self-Organization Checklist

1. Write down your assignments.

2. Follow all directions.

3. Keep all your materials together.

4. Use special parts of textbooks—table of contents, index, and glossary—for preliminary information.

5. Read chapters for main ideas.

6. Read each paragraph.

7. Think how to group ideas and sequence.

8. Decide what the main idea is.

9. Place check marks by supporting details.

10. Group ideas together (categories).

11. Determine sequence—order tells a story.

12. Create an outline.

13. Create a map, a type of outline that looks like a picture.

14. Use a graph to organize information.

15. Create or follow a diagram—any picture that helps teach or explain.

16. Make a timeline.

17. Underline or highlight important information.

18. Collect information from books or the Internet.

19. Write down and look up new words.

20. Keep a dictionary near to clarify words.

21. Use illustrations to add to your report.

22. Set a goal and timeline for your project.

23. Do the hardest assignment first.

24. Take a break.

LESSON 11-C

....

Topic Generation

To the Instructor ....

Students are unsure of what they should research, read, or write about. The more the topic fits the student, the better the finished results will be.

Objectives ....

1. Students learn topic-generation techniques to help them choose a subject to research.

2. Students learn to work from the general to the specific, revising their topic as they go.

3. Students learn how to use graphic organizers to further refine their topic.

Materials ....

Transparencies

11.3 Topic Generation ☐ ◨ ■

11.4 Look at the Whole Story ☐ ◨ ■

Lists of suggested topics
Graphic organizer worksheets

Teaching and Preparation ....

1. Discuss the importance of choosing a topic for a research project.

2. Demonstrate various topic-generation techniques.

3. Explain how a person works from topic generation to finished product.

4. Review Internet references.

   www.lib.csusb.edu/history/unit1/tutorial1/u1t1p3topic%20generation.htm

   www.pcguide.com/topic.html

Worksheet ....

11.2 Resource Evaluation Table □ ◧ ■

Connections to the Curriculum ....

Students need to choose topics in all subjects for research papers.

Answer Key ....

WORKSHEET 11.2

Answers will vary.

Topic Generation

Anything can be the topic you will research. Topics need to be refined from the general to the specific to avoid having too much information to make a good finished product.

Finding Topics

Brainstorming   Talking with a group of students to help you think about topics.

Clustering   Grouping the topics that are alike.

Free writing   Brainstorming by an individual in which he or she writes down anything that comes to mind that might make a good topic.

List making   Writing down anything that you think of that might make a good topic for the assignment.

Organizing questions   Asking yourself the following: What are the things I know about the topic? What are the things I don't know about the topic? What are the things I would like to know about the topic? and Where can I find information about the topic?

Teacher generating a list of topics   Having the instructor supply subjects that are essential to learning the curriculum.

Guidelines

1. Pick topics that are fun and interesting.
2. Select a topic that meets the requirements of your assignment.
3. Choose topics related to what you are studying.
4. Give yourself plenty of time to research.
5. Locate materials in the library media center before completing your choice of topic.
6. Be sure materials are available and there are enough of them to do your work in one place.
7. Keep good notes on cards or in a notebook.
8. Don't be afraid to change or alter your topic because the resource materials are not confirming your ideas.
9. Make a list of related words that might provide information about your topic.

Possible Topics

1. Use the Dewey Classification System information for general topic areas.
2. Keep a notebook of topic ideas for future reference.
3. Topic Suggestions:

   • Animals • Archaeology • Art • Astronomy • Awards • Business • Cities • Computers • Countries
   • Disease • Drugs • Education • Economics • Elections • Entertainment • Environment • Events • Family
   • Food • Games • Government • Health • Heroes • History • Holidays • Inventions • Languages • Law
   • Leaders • Literature • Military • Movies • Music • Newspapers • Outdoors • People • Photography
   • Planets • Plants • Recreation • Sports • States • Transportation • Travel • Vacations • Weather
   • Wildlife • World

TRANSPARENCY 11.3

Requirements for Topic Generation for a Paper or Project

1. Three parts to paper or project

    All levels (beginning, grades 3 and 4; intermediate, grades 5 and 6; and advanced, grades 7 and 8) are required to have an introduction, body, and conclusion.

    Introduction = give point of view
    Body = prove points, supply examples and quotations
    Conclusion = summarize points, restate main idea

2. Length of project or paper

    Beginning: two to four sentences
    Intermediate: two to four paragraphs
    Advanced: two to four pages or more, depending on ability, time, and topic

3. Information requirements

    Beginning: two to four resources—encyclopedia, dictionary, Internet, topic book, magazine

    Intermediate: four to eight resources—encyclopedia, dictionary, Internet, topic books, magazines, newspapers

    Advanced: eight or more resources—encyclopedia, dictionary, Internet, topic books, magazines, newspapers, CD-ROMs, electronic media, interviews

4. Bibliography

    Beginning: only onsite materials
    Intermediate: resources onsite and outside of building
    Advanced: bibliography using formal guidelines for all resources

5. Finished project

    Beginning: handwritten or computer-printed paper
    Intermediate: handwritten, computer-printed paper, or oral presentation
    Advanced: handwritten, computer-printed paper, or oral and/or media presentation

 **TRANSPARENCY 11.3 cont.**

Look at the Whole Story

How do you evaluate resources?
Gather, Compare, Contrast, Eliminate

Gather

1. Develop questions and topics from instructor guidelines.

2. List the requirements and information needed to complete the project.

3. Decide what is important and write your own questions.

4. Locate information in more than one format (book, video, Internet).

5. Find information that demonstrates agreement between resources.

6. Look for materials from creditable authors who are experts in their fields.

7. Use materials that are readily available. Don't use a book that everyone else wants or is in a library you can't go to.

8. Select materials appropriate to your intelligence level (number of pages, indexes, illustrations).

Compare, Contrast, Eliminate

9. Organize the resources and information in a table for easy evaluation.

10. Choose the best resources by comparing the information.

    A. The resources that best fit the topic information requirements and answer the questions

    B. The resources with the best organization, and that are easy to use and understand

11. Rank the materials by usefulness.

12. Return the eliminated and unnecessary materials.

13. Write a bibliography for the resources you will use in your project.

NAME _____   DATE _____

Resource Evaluation Table

Directions: Use this form to evaluate and refine your topic selection.

Title/Format	Organization	Usefulness of Information	Location	Topics and Subtopics Covered	Supporting Materials	Questions and Requirements Covered

LESSON 11-D

....

Note Taking

To the Instructor ....

How many times have you asked students "Are you writing this down?" Students should learn to take notes in lectures and classes. They also need to know how to write notes for print and electronic media.

Objectives ....

1. Students learn the procedures for taking notes in the classroom.

2. Students develop skills to take notes for doing independent research.

Materials ....

Transparency

11.5 Tips for Note Taking □ ◧ ■

Various resources students would use to do research projects
Online computer

Teaching and Preparation ....

1. Demonstrate how to take notes in lectures, from texts and research books, and from the Internet.

2. Conduct a short lecture for students to develop note-writing skills.

3. Critique the notes for components to do a report.

4. Review Internet references.

   http://www.iss.stthomas.edu/studyguides/booknote.htm

   www.csbsju.edu/academicadvising/help/lec-note.html

   http://www.how-to-study.com

Activities ....

Students will take notes from print and electronic media, and from lectures. (no page) □ ◨ ■

The librarian will help critique note taking. (no page) ◨ ■

Worksheet ....

11.3 Listening □ ◨ ■

Connections to the Curriculum ....

Note taking is a necessity for all the curriculum areas.

Answer Key ....

WORKSHEET 11.3

Answers will vary.

Tips for Note Taking

The goal is to understand what you are listening to or reading.

General

1. Develop a strategy, and your own style.

2. Be consistent.

3. Eliminate distractions.

4. Don't try to write everything that is said.

5. Copy everything, or the most important things, on the blackboard, transparencies, and so on.

6. Work quickly.

7. Summarize in your own words.

8. Use abbreviations.

9. Use examples and sketches.

10. Use a separate notebook for each class or assignment with writing on only one side of the paper.

11. Look for signal words.

    These are reasons

    First, second, third

    And most important

    A major development

    For example

    Similarly

12. Look for transition words.

    Therefore

    In conclusion

    As a result

    Finally

13. Ask questions for items that need clarification.

 **TRANSPARENCY 11.5**

Print

1. Write questions that need to be answered before beginning to read.

2. Read the material first for understanding.

3. Read only a section or paragraph at a time for answers to questions.

4. Locate main ideas and supporting information.

5. Don't copy everything.

6. Put information into your own words.

7. Write only enough to understand.

8. Write a bibliography of the books you used for your research and keep with your notes.

Lecture/classroom

1. Read and review text and outside reading assignments before the lecture or class.

2. Copy boards and transparencies.

3. Watch the speaker carefully.

4. Be brief in note taking.

5. Summarize in your own words.

Electronic (Internet, audiotapes, videotapes, television)

1. Write questions you want to answer.

2. Access information on the Internet or in other electronic forms.

3. Listen and look intently.

4. Read and look.

5. Locate main ideas and supporting details.

6. Put information into your own words.

7. Write only enough to understand.

8. Write a bibliography of the Internet sites, tapes, or shows you used for your research and keep it with your notes.

Listening

Directions: Use this form to guide you in taking notes from a lecture or class.

Write the topic:_____

Write the speaker's name: _____

List collaborating materials named as resources:

_____

_____

_____

List important facts learned from the lecture:

_____

_____

_____

_____

1. Did you understand how all of the facts fit together to explain a process? Y/N:

   A. Write notes and ask any questions when the speaker is finished.

2. Did the speaker use any words or expressions that are unfamiliar to you? Y/N:

   A. If yes, list the words and ask the speaker to define them. Don't worry about the spelling.

3. Do you think the speaker could improve the content of the report in any way? Y/N:

   A. If yes, write your suggestions.

LESSON 11-E

Prewriting

To the Instructor

Students need help in organizing their thoughts to write any assignment.

Objectives

1. Students learn about different prewriting techniques.

2. Students learn how to decide which prewriting techniques best serve different writing assignments.

3. Students understand how to choose prewriting techniques that best serve their individual learning styles.

Materials

Transparency

11.6 Prewriting Techniques ☐ ◨ ■

Information about the various prewriting techniques
Different books and articles for practice

Teaching and Preparation ....

1. Demonstrate how to use each prewriting technique.

2. Display different books and articles for the students to choose the best prewriting technique to use to write a good report.

3. Review Internet references.

   www.kcmetro.cc.mo.us/maplewoods/writeplace/techniquescreating.html

   www.whsd.k12.pa.us/wh/Teachers/Arthla/writing_process.htm

   http://www.angelfire.com/wi/writingprocess/prewriting.html

   http://www.bartleby.com/141/

Activity ....

Students will practice with short articles from magazines or newspapers to organize their thoughts. (no page) □ ◧ ■

Connections to the Curriculum ....

All areas of the curriculum can use the prewriting techniques to organize information before writing assignments and reports.

Prewriting Techniques

Gather your ideas and use one of the following activities to decide on your written work.

Brainstorm   A close cousin of free writing; to capture fleeting ideas and words, fragments, and sometimes sentences. Brainstorming on a topic or subject yields a set of words, fragments, and occasionally sentences. The ideas sometimes look irrelevant. As you write you will combine, modify, and omit some of the notes.

Cluster   To put like ideas into groups and look at them as topics and subtopics.

Draw   To make pictures of ideas or subjects.

Free writing   To snare thoughts as they race through your mind. First write the sentences and then look them over for ideas. Write for five minutes on your general subject. Don't worry about grammar, spelling, or punctuation.

Keep a journal   To record your experiences in a notebook. There is freedom to explore thought, feelings, responses, attitudes, and beliefs. It is private and there is no worry of doing it right or wrong. Write in any kind of notebook. Write on a regular basis at least five minutes at a time.

Mapping   See Webs.

Sort out a subject   To break broad subjects into categories and subcategories. Once done, look over the ideas and see what topics turn up.

Taping your reading   To use a personal tape recorder and talk your ideas into dated information sources. It is especially good for family memories, discussions, and the like.

Webs   To draw organizing circles with the main topic in the middle, with all subtopics radiating from the center.

LESSON 11-F

Basic Outlining

To the Instructor ....

Students need a way to organize the information they found doing research.

Objectives ....

1. Students learn the standard outline format.

2. Students learn how to use the standard outline format to organize data for reports in a logical sequence.

Materials ....

Transparency

11.7 Basic Outline Form □ ◧ ■

A short article or story to practice outlining

Teaching and Preparation ....

1. Demonstrate an outlining example.

2. Work through a sample outline with a familiar story or article.

3. Review Internet references.

   http://www.lib.jjay.cuny.edu/research/outlining.html

Activities ....

Use the sample outline to create a practice outline. (no page) ☐ ◧ ■

Create an outline for a class assignment. (no page) ☐ ◧ ■

Connections to the Curriculum ....

Outlining is necessary in all areas of the curriculum.

Basic Outline Form

Outline   A picture of the main ideas, topics, subsidiary ideas, and subtopics of any subject. It is a basic overview of a subject, and the important ideas are listed using roman numerals, alphabet letters, and Arabic letters for organization and easy viewing.

Main idea (topic)   The key concepts.

Subsidiary ideas (subtopics)   The supporting, additional, and further information (details).

Arabic numerals   1 = one, 2 = two, and so on.

Roman numerals   I = one, V = five, X = ten, and so on.

1. First, brainstorm; second, read and take notes; third, organize your data in outline form by deciding on the main idea, subsidiary ideas, and so on.

2. Use full sentences or phrases.

3. List in chronological order.

4. Change and reorder as necessary.

5. If there is a *one* then there is a *two,* if there is an *A* then there is a *B,* and so on.

Outline Sample

I.   Main Idea

   A. Subtopic

   B. Subtopic

      1. Additional idea

      2. Additional idea

         a. Further idea

         b. Further idea

II. Main Idea

Timeline

To the Instructor

How many times have you asked students about the order of events in a story? Students should be able to use a tool to organize their thoughts in a chronological order. The timeline is the perfect visual means.

Objectives

1. Students understand the graphic organizer of a timeline.

2. Students learn how to construct a list of dates and accompanying information.

3. Students learn how to organize data on a horizontal or vertical line with accompanying information.

Materials

Transparency

11.8 Timeline □ ◧ ■

Historical material with dates
Fictional story with time-passing information

Teaching and Preparation . . . .

1. Demonstrate how to construct and arrange information on a timeline.

2. Review Internet references.

   http://www.sbrowning.com/whowhatwhen/

   http://www.smartdraw.com

   htttp://www.timelines.info

Connections to the Curriculum . . . .

Social studies teachers use the timeline to help students understand the relationships of different events to the continuum of time.

Timeline

A timeline is a graphic way of looking at information.

It can be a horizontal line with tick marks or other ways of showing year changes.

It may also be a list of dates and accompanying information. A measurement such as one inch on the timeline equals a specified number of years.

All the events in history cannot be shown on one timeline. A person must choose a subject to display.

Line Construction

1. Choose a subject and collect data.

2. Organize the data you want to display.

3. Decide on the time intervals.

4. Decide on the legend information.

5. Draw a horizontal line with the time intervals.

6. Place the dates and caption information below the line in a relevant position.

7. Place "breaks" on the line to skip years where nothing of major importance to the subject happened and that would not add to the relevance of the timeline.

Timeline Rules

1. B.C. years are before the birth of Christ.

2. A.D. years are after the birth of Christ.

3. For historical events, the years are larger at the ends than in the middle if there is a "0" used.

4. For a person's life, the years begin with birth at "0" on the left and continue to the right.

Sample

One inch equals five years.

0	5
Born	Kindergarten
1994	2000

5. To show years passing that are not relevant to the subject of the timeline, place a break in the line.

6. To find "time passed" on a timeline:

   A. If the dates are B.C. and A.D., add the dates on the timeline together.

   B. If the dates are B.C. and B.C. or A.D and A.D., subtract one date from the other.

7. Centuries begin with 0 on the timeline, and 0 to 99 is century one; 100 to 199 is century two. To determine in which century an event occurred, add one to the first part of the year: 399 would be the fourth century; 1999 would be the twentieth century.

LESSON 11-H

Draft Writing

To the Instructor

Are your students interested in writing or changing a paper more than one time? The teacher and librarian's responsibility is to make the student understand the value of doing quality work capable of being published, and to provide the tools to make rewriting a part of the process.

Objectives

1. Students learn to use the draft writing checklist (Transparency 11.10) to organize their written assignments.

2. Students learn to use highlighting as part of recognizing the need to change their first efforts. They understand how to choose sentences out of long paragraphs that contain the most important information, and learn to paraphrase information.

Materials

Transparencies

11.9 Draft Writing ☐ ◼ ◼

11.10 Draft Writing Checklist ☐ ◼ ◼

Highlighters or light-colored markers
Student work

Teaching and Preparation ....

1. Demonstrate how to choose what and when to highlight.

2. Use proofreader's marks on selected copy.

3. Review Internet reference.

    http://www.finaldraft.com

Connections to the Curriculum ....

All subject teachers should have copies of the Draft Writing Checklist to develop consistent skills in written work.

Draft Writing

1. As you develop your final copy, check to see if you have included the following:

    A. A beginning, middle, and end

    B. Paragraphs

    C. A controlling idea

    D. A progression in logical order

    E. Transitions, repetition, pronouns, and parallel structure between and within paragraphs

    F. Elaboration through relevant details and examples

    G. Vivid language

    H. Sentences that are clear and varied in structure

    I. Writing techniques such as imagery, humor, point of view, voice

    J. Complexity, freshness of thought, and individual perspective

    K. Awareness of audience and purpose

    L. Few errors in grammar, usage, punctuation, capitalization, and spelling

2. Ask a peer to read your paper and make suggestions.

3. Revise, edit, and rewrite.

4. Add pictures and other media to enhance your written work.

5. Publish.

Draft Writing Checklist

1. **Plan**
   Ask questions of your teacher and yourself so you know what the assignment really is.

2. **Understand the topic**
   List ideas and things you already know about the subject.

3. **Gather information**
   Use research books, encyclopedias, the Internet, and so on.

4. **Organize**
   Use the prewriting techniques: outline, narrow the topic.

5. **Develop a thesis**
   Ask yourself what you want to say about the subject.

6. **Make a first draft**
   Type or write your ideas using your prewriting information.

7. **Revise**
   Change and add sentences to make sense.

8. **Proofread**
   Look for all errors of grammar, spelling, and wrong information.

9. **Select a title**

10. **Ask for peer evaluation**
    Ask friends to read your paper and make suggestions.

11. **Make a final draft**
    Use a word processor with spell check and grammar check. Check the font for readability. Place the paper in a folder for presentation.

TRANSPARENCY 11.10

LESSON 11-1

Publishing

To the Instructor

How does the student's finished writing look? Has the student checked to see if anything was forgotten? Now is the time to put all the information from this book into a finished product.

Objectives

1. Student's work will not have any grammar or spelling errors.

2. Student's work will look like a published book.

3. A students' corner in the library will have works done by students.

Materials

Transparency

   11.11 Publishing Checklist ☐ ◧ ■

Examples of published authors' work and students' work

Teaching and Preparation . . . .

1. Display students' finished work and compare it to other authors' works in the library's collection.

2. Review Internet references.

   http://www.kidscom.com/create/write/write.html

   www.kidauthors.com/

   www.liswa.wa.gov.au/funhouse/kidswrit.htm

Connections to the Curriculum . . . .

Students and teachers should have projects and papers that others would like to see. This is an opportunity to display students' accomplishments in writing. When they make covers and dust jackets, they are also showing artistic talents.

Publishing Checklist

The book should include the following:

1. A cover

2. A title page

3. A copyright page

4. A contents page

5. A body of work

6. A glossary

7. An index

8. A bibliography

9. An about the author page

10. An about the book page

The dust jacket should include the following:

1. An about the author note

2. An about the book summary or tease

3. An artistic cover

4. Spine information for placing the book on the library shelves

 **TRANSPARENCY 11.11**

The Children's Literature Lover's Book of Lists

Joanna Sullivan

Paperback/ 386 pages
ISBN: 0-7879-6595-2

"Joanna's book is clearly written, needed—and most important—has a friendly layout so that teachers (and parents) are able to find good resources for children. The direct, to-the-point way that she's constructed it will lure an audience to keep thumbing through it."

—Susan Mandel Glazer, professor of graduate studies, Rider University and past president of the International Reading Association

This unique book is written for teachers, parents, librarians, and anyone who is seeking quality literature for children (preschoolers through grade 6). The book is filled with wide-ranging lists of titles organized by grade level, theme, and content areas. This comprehensive resource simplifies your search by selecting the most useful information from Websites, teacher resources, award listings, and publications that are available on children's literature.

For quick access and easy use, the lists are printed in full-page format and organized into five sections:

Section One—Books for Pre-K through Grade 1: Contains favorite classics, wordless picture books, read-alouds, concept books, animal stories, folk and fairy tales, and books about music, science, math, sports, and more.
Section Two—Books for Grades 2 and 3: Includes all time favorites, multicultural themes, biographies of historical figures, sports heroes, reference books, and books to help teach poetry.
Section Three—Books for Grades 4 through 6: Offers biographies, historical fiction, poetry, science fiction, legends, and realistic fiction on social topics.
Section Four—Children's Book Awards and Recommended Literature: Consists of lists of children's book award winners and recommendations from such groups and organizations as the New York Public Library, the American Library Association, and the International Reading Association.
Section Five—Children's Literature Websites and Teacher Resources: Contains online information about children's literature, teacher resources, magazines, and other Websites.

Joanna Sullivan is director of the Family Literacy Program for Migrant Workers, affiliated with Southern Illinois University in Carbondale. Dr. Sullivan has taught reading, children's literature, and language arts at Pennsylvania State University and Florida Atlantic University, and was director of the Reading Clinic at Fairleigh Dickinson University in Teaneck, New Jersey.

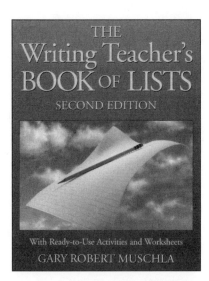

The Writing Teachers Book of Lists, 2nd Edition
with Ready-to-Use Activities and Worksheets

Gary Robert Muschla

Paperback/ 368 pages
ISBN: 0-7879-7080-8

This is the second edition of the unique information source and timesaver for English and language arts teachers. *The Writing Teacher's Book of Lists with Ready-to-Use Activities and Worksheets* includes ninety useful lists for developing instructional materials and planning lessons for elementary and secondary students. In addition, the book includes innovative activities and reproducible black-line masters that help students to improve their writing skills, word usage, and vocabulary.

For quick access and easy use, all of these lists and activities are organized into seven sections and individually printed in a format that can be photocopied as many times as required for individual or group instruction. This handy resource is filled with helpful lists, activities, teaching suggestions, and reproducible worksheets.

Lists and Activities for Special Words and Word Groups: Contains the information students need on topics such as synonyms, antonyms, hard-to-spell words, easily confused words, and words associated with time.

Lists and Activities for Nonfiction Writing: Aids students in their understanding of nonfiction topics including advertising, ecology, education, government and politics, newspapers and magazines, sciences, and travel.
Lists and Activities for Fiction Writing

Lists and Activities for Writing Style

Rules, "Check" Lists, and Activities for Student Writers

Special Lists for Student Writers

Special Lists for Teachers

Gary Robert Muschla, B.A., M.A.T., taught reading and writing for more than twenty-five years at Appleby School in Spotswood, New Jersey. He is the author of several practical resources for teachers, including *Writing Workshop Survival Kit, English Teacher's Great Books Activities Kit, Reading Workshop Survival Kit,* and three books of *Ready-to-Use Reading Proficiency Lessons and Activities,* 4th-, 8th-, and 10th-Grade levels, all published by Jossey-Bass.

Listen to Learn:
Using American Music to Understand Language Arts and Social Studies (Grades 5–8), with CD

Teri Tibbett

Paperback/ 464 pages
ISBN: 0-7879-7254-1

A new approach to using music to provide engaging and thematically linked activities for middle school teachers in language arts and social studies. This practical, easy-to-use activities book offers a way for middle school teachers to capture students' interest through musical links to standards-driven lessons. With the accompanying CD, each unit offers an exciting activity and learning experience that includes historical information and cultural insight, enhances reading and comprehension skills, and inspires creativity and a love of music. Activities cover American music from a variety of cultural backgrounds, from Native American music to rock, rap, jazz, folk, classical, and more.

Teri Tibbett lives in Anchorage, Alaska and has taught music to all grades throughout the state since 1976, both as an itinerant music teacher and through her own school, The Juneau School of Creative Arts.

The Vocabulary Teacher's Book of Lists

Edward B. Fry, Ph.D.

Paper/ 352 pages
ISBN: 0-7879-7101-4

A fun way to teach tricky vocabulary rules
to students at all levels!

Designed to assist the reading or language arts teacher with spelling and vocabulary building—as well as engage in some of the more whimsical uses of language—this book focuses on particularly troublesome words. Along with various sections dealing with homographs and heteronyms, the book also covers easily confused words, prefixes, spelling demons, word families, roots, homophones, and more. Not at all dull and dry, it employs clever and fun language usage, including a complete section addressing puns and wordplay. The author also includes teaching suggestions for special populations of students.

Edward Bernard Fry, Ph.D. (Laguna Beach, California), is professor emeritus of education at Rutgers University, where for twenty-four years he was director of the Reading Center. He is the author of the best-selling *Reading Teacher's Book of Lists,* now in its fourth edition and the renowned inventor of Fry's Readability Graph.

Paving the Way in Reading and Writing:
Strategies and Activities to Support Struggling Students in Grades 6–12

Larry G. Lewin

Paper/ 272 pages
ISBN: 0-7879-6414-X

"Lewin's emphasis on effective instruction that integrates both reading and writing offers me just what I want most from a book: useful classroom strategies based on both research and master teacher's experience with real kids. . . . a welcome addition to my toolbox of useful books."

—**Jim Burke, author,** *The English Teacher's Companion: A Complete Guide to Classroom, Curriculum, and the Profession* **and** *The Reader's Handbook: A Student Guide for Reading and Learning*

Paving the Way in Reading and Writing offers secondary teachers from across the content areas a structured approach for motivating reluctant and disengaged students to tackle difficult reading and writing assignments and thus boost their potential for academic success. Drawing on relevant theory and research and the author's extensive experience as a teacher and teacher trainer, the book presents an arsenal of practical instructional strategies along with teacher-tested tools, techniques, and activities for helping students improve their comprehension of informational and literary text as well as strengthen their written communications. Activities combining reading and writing tasks are emphasized along with graphic exercises for engaging the more visually oriented students. The book also provides guidance on using the computer as a literacy tool and on improving students' grammar, spelling, and research skills. In addition, it offers extensive listings of Web-based instructional resources.

Larry Lewin, a former teacher, is author of numerous books on teaching practice and consults nationally to school districts on professional development topics.

English Teacher's Survival Guide:
Ready-to-Use Techniques & Materials For Grades 7–12

Mary Lou Brandvik

Paper/ 245 pages
ISBN: 0-13-045681-0

Practice the art of teaching English effectively and leave labor-intensive ways behind with the *English Teacher's Survival Guide.*

- Devise a fair grading system
- Create a positive design for discipline
- Delegate tasks to students that can become learning experiences for them and time savers for you
- Arrange the room for efficient classroom management . . . and more.

Included are 175 easy-to-use strategies, lessons, and checklists for effective classroom management, and over 50 reproducible samples that you can adopt immediately for planning, evaluation, or assignments. The guide helps you create a classroom that reflects the excitement for learning that every English teacher desires.

Mary Lou Brandvik was graduated summa cum laude from Concordia College in Moorhead, Minnesota, with a B.A. in English and art. She also earned a Masters degree from the University of Illinois. Ms. Brandvik has taught in public schools in Illinois and Minnesota, as well as at Bemidji State University in Minnesota. She was named the 1988 Teacher of the Year of the Bemidji Pubic Schools and in 1991 received the Lila B. Wallace Teacher-Scholar Award from the National Endowment for the Humanities. She is also the author of *Writing Process Activities Kit,* published by The Center for Applied Research in Education.